Basic Swedish Grammar

Ann-Mari Beite

Gertrud Englund

Siv Higelin

Nils-Gustav Hildeman

Almqvist & Wiksell Läromedel

Publications by
The Institute for English-Speaking Students
University of Stockholm · Sweden

The Institute for English-Speaking Students at the University of Stockholm offers one-year courses for social science graduates at the International Graduate School and Scandinavian area courses for undergraduates at the Stockholm Junior Year. All instruction is given in English. Both departments offer courses in the Swedish language. The University of Stockholm also offers a special Master's degree for foreign students. Separate courses in the Swedish language are also offered by the Institute.

The Institute for English-Speaking Students · University of Stockholm
Fiskartorpsvägen 160 E · 104 05 Stockholm 50 · Sweden

© 1963 Ann-Mari Beite, Gertrud Englund, Siv Higelin, Nils-Gustav Hildeman and Almqvist & Wiksell Läromedel AB, Stockholm

Third edition
7

Printed in Sweden by
Gotab, Stockholm 1980

ISBN 91-21-01551-1

Publications by
The Institute for English-Speaking Students
University of Stockholm   Sweden

Preface

"Basic Swedish Grammar" is a systematic grammar designed as the complement of a textbook for the beginner's study of the Swedish language.

The aim of the authors has been to provide a grammar presenting modern Swedish. The book is meant to be used in a practical teaching situation; for this reason we have attempted to give simple and clear explanations rather than complete analyses of grammatical problems.

In an appendix are listed some words that present difficulties of translation to English-speaking students.

"Basic Swedish Grammar" was compiled by the following authors Ann-Mari Beite, Gertrud Englund, Siv Higelin and Nils-Gustav Hildeman. It was edited by Ann-Mari Beite.

At the Stockholm University Institute for English-Speaking Students Basic Swedish Grammar is used together with the reader "Learn Swedish" (Almqvist & Wiksell) and "Practise Swedish" (Almqvist & Wiksell).

In the third edition some alterations have been made, notably in the chapter dealing with the use of the indefinite and definite declensions of the adjective, in the introduction to the main verbs, in the passage on compound verbs (a commentary on the place of the separable part of a compound verb has been added), and in the passage on the place of the adverb where a few examples have been added.

The Editor

Contents

SWEDISH PRONUNCIATION

It is not possible to acquire an accurate pronunciation of a foreign language through written instruction. In the following chapter, however, are given some main principles for the pronunciation of Swedish and comments on Swedish vowel and consonant sounds compared to those of other languages, which may prove helpful to students studying the language on their own. The chapter must be supplemented by oral instruction, from a teacher or from gramophone records.

Note. When sounds in Swedish are compared to those of other languages the similarity is always approximative.

The Alphabet

1 There are three more letters in the Swedish alphabet than in the English. These are the vowels Å Ä Ö. They are placed at the end of the alphabet:

A B C D E F G H I J K L M N O P Q R S T U V W X Y Z Å Ä Ö

In modern Swedish the consonants Q and W are used only in names of persons (e.g. Wilhelm Söderqvist) and places and in a few loan words. Words beginning with W are listed in dictionaries among words beginning with V, not after them.

2 A O U Å can be called *hard vowels*.
E I Y Ä Ö can be called *soft vowels*.

This distinction is important for explaining the different pronunciations of the consonants *g*, *k* and the consonant combination *sk* before different vowels.

Stress

A syllable can be stressed or unstressed.
3 In Swedish words the principal stress is generally on the *first* syllable:

skola *school*   alltid *always*   bagare *baker*

Note. The difference in stress between a stressed and an unstressed syllable is smaller in Swedish than in English. Even an unstressed syllable should be pronounced distinctly in Swedish. This is important for instance for the pronunciation of final vowels.

Compare the names

   Anna *Anne*   Eva *Eve*   Rosa *Rose*

4   Words whose principal stress is not on the first syllable are often of foreign origin. Such are for instance

1. words with the prefixes *be-*, *ge-* and (usually) *för-* (of German origin). The stress is on the syllable following the prefix:

   betala *pay*   gemensam *common*   förstå *understand*

2. words of French or Latin origin, which usually have the stress on the last syllable:

   universitet *university*   polis *policeman*   cigarrett *cigarette*

Vowels

Quantity

The Swedish vowels are either long or short.

5   1. In **stressed syllables** the vowel is almost always **long** if it is

a) the final vowel in words of one syllable:

   ja *yes*   sko *shoe*   nu *now*   två *two*
   tre *three*   vi *we*   ny *new*   trä *wood*   snö *snow*

b) followed by *one* consonant:

   glas *glass*   bok *book*   hus *house*   båt *boat*
   brev *letter*   fin *fine*   dyr *expensive*   väg *way*   hög *high*
   Note, however, the case of *M* and *N* mentioned below in 2. and in § 15.

2. In **stressed syllables** the vowel is usually **short** if it is followed by *more than one* consonant (it is always short when followed by a double consonant):

   arm *arm*   ost *cheese*   buss *bus*   gått *gone*
   svensk *Swedish*   film *film*   rygg *back*   vägg *wall*   höst *autumn*

M and *N* at the end of words are usually not doubled in spelling, even though the preceding vowel is short. The vowel is short in for instance:

hem *home* om *if* rum *room* vem *who*[m]
en *a, an, one* han *he* hon *she* den *it*
See further § 15.

6 In **unstressed syllables** the vowel is *always* **short.** Note, however, that even the unstressed vowels are pronounced distinctly in Swedish and are not, as often in English, reduced to a murmur vowel:

flicka *girl* gammal *old* syster *sister*

Quality

The Swedish vowels are pure vowels and not diphthongs. Compare for instance the pronunciation of English "go" and Swedish "gå".

7 **Hard Vowels**

a The *long* vowel represented by *a* resembles the *a* in English "father":

dag *day* glas *glass* par *pair* gata *street* bara *only*

The *short* vowel resembles the *a* in French "salle", German "Sache":

arm *arm* gammal *old* glass *ice-cream* kaffe *coffee*

o The letter *o* represents *two* different sounds:

1. A long vowel resembling *oo* in English "moon", *ou* in French "fou":

bok *book* stor *big* stol *chair* ropa *cry*

A short vowel resembling *oo* in English "book", *ou* in French "boule"

blomma *flower* moster *aunt* ost *cheese*

2. The same vowel sound as that represented by the vowel *å* for which see below.

u The *long* sound represented by *u* is a half-close front vowel pronounced with strong lip rounding:

du *you* ful *ugly* hus *house* nu *now*

The *short* vowel is pronounced with less strong lip rounding:

buss *bus* full *full* gubbe *old man*

å The *long* vowel represented by *å* resembles *eau* in French "beau", *o* in German "Sohn": This sound can also be spelled with *o*:

då *then*   båt *boat*   son *son*   sova *sleep*   två *two*

The *short* sound resembles *o* in British English "lost", French "voler", German "Sonne". This sound can also be spelled with *o*:

doktor *doctor*   komma *come*   kopp *cup*   måste *must*

8 Soft Vowels

e The *long* vowel represented by *e* resembles the *é* in French "été", *ee* in German "See":

bred *broad*   brev *letter*   resa *travel*   tre *three*

The *short* sound resembles *e* in English "get":

ett *a, an, one*   penna *pencil*   svensk *Swedish*

i The *long* vowel represented by *i* resembles *i* in English "machine" German "hier", French "puni":

bil *car*   fin *fine*   vi *we*   visa *show*

The *short* sound resembles *i* in French "mine", German "finden":

film *film*   inte *not*   sitta *sit*   viss *certain*

y The *long* vowel represented by *y* resembles the *u* in French "mur" and the *ü* in German "über":

sy *sew*   dyr *expensive*   fyra *four*   ny *new*

The *short* sound resembles the *u* in French "lune" and *ü* in German "füllen":

nyckel *key*   rygg *back*   syster *sister*

ä The letter *ä* represents *two* different sounds:
  1. '*ä*' *before consonants other than* '*r*' *or at the end of words.*
     The *long* vowel resembles *ê* in French "fête", German *ä* in "Jäger":

     väder *weather*   träd *tree*   väg *way*   äta *eat*   trä *wood*

     The *short* sound in large parts of Sweden is the same as the short e-sound (English "get", "best"):

     bäst *best*   vägg *wall*   äpple *apple*

2. *'ä' before 'r'.* The vowel is more open in this position.
The *long* sound resembles *è* in French "mère":

där *there*   här *here*   lära *teach*   päron *pear*

The *short* sound resembles the first *e* in French "verte":

lärka *lark*   märka *notice*

ö The letter *ö* represents *two* different sounds:

1. *'ö' before consonants other than 'r'* or at the end of words
The *long* sound resembles *eu* in French "feu", *ö* in German "Söhne":

hög *high*   snö *snow*   öga *eye*

The *short* sound resembles *eu* in French "seul", *ö* in German "öffnen":

fönster *window*   höst *autumn*   öppen *open*

2. *'ö' before 'r'.* The vowel is more open in this position.
The *long* sound resembles *e* in English "her", *eu* in French "peur":

höra *hear*   öra *ear*

The short sound resembles *eu* in French "heurter":

dörr *door*   förr *before*   mörk *dark*

Consonants

9 Some consonants represent almost the same sounds in Swedish and in
English. This applies primarily to the consonants *b, f, h, m, p, v.* The
consonants *q, w* and *z* represent the same sounds as *k, v* and *s* respectively.

Pronunciation of g, k and sk

10 *The letters 'g', 'k' and the consonant combination 'sk' sometimes represent
the same sounds as in English and sometimes different sounds, depending
on the following vowel.*

A. g, k, and **sk** are pronounced as in English 'gate, Kate, skate'

1. before the hard vowels (*a, o, u, ǫ*):

   gammal *old*   god *good*   gul *yellow*   gå *go, walk*
   katt *cat*   ko *cow*   kust *coast*   kål *cabbage*
   skatt *tax*   sko *shoe*   skur *shower*   skål *toast*

2. before consonants:

   gnaga *gnaw*   grön *green*   glas *glass*
   kläder *clothes*   kniv *knife*   krona *crown*
   skriva *write*

3. before *e* and *i* in unstressed syllables:

   skogen *the wood*   dragig *draughty*
   boken *the book*   tråkig *boring*
   asken *the box*   ruskig *disgusting*

4. at the end of words:

   skog *forest*   (see also below B, note.)
   bok *book*
   ask *box*

B. Before the soft vowels (*e i y ä ö*) in stressed syllables

g is pronounced like *y* in English "yellow", *j* in German "Jahr":

   ge *give*   gift *married*   gynna *favour*   gärna *gladly*   göra *do*

k is pronounced like *ch* in German 'ich':

   kedja *chain*   Kina *China*   kyrka *church*   kär *dear*   köpa *buy*

sk represents several sounds which are similar but vary with different persons. Some use a sound resembling *sh* in English 'show':

   sked *spoon*   skida *ski*   skynda *hurry*   skära *cut*   sköta *handle*

Note. **g** has its "soft" pronunciation finally after *l* and *r*:

   helg *holiday*   älg *elk, moose*
   berg *mountain*   torg *square*   Göteborg *Gothenburg*

Other spellings of these sounds

1 The same sounds as those represented by *g*, *k* and *sk* before soft vowels can be spelled in many different ways.

A. Like "*soft*" *g* ("yellow", "Jahr") are pronounced:

1. The letter **j**: ja *yes*   jord *earth*   jul *Christmas*   böja *bend*

2. The combinations **dj, gj, hj,** and **lj** at the beginning of words or in compound words when these consonants belong to the same syllable:

djup *deep*   djur *animal*   djärv *bold*
gjorde *did*   gjort *done*
hjord *herd*   hjul *wheel*   hjärta *heart*   hjärna *brains*
ljud *sound*   ljus *light*   ljuga *lie*

Thus there is no difference of pronunciation between:
jord – hjord, jul – hjul, gärna – hjärna

B. Like "*soft*" *k* ("ich") are pronounced:

The combinations **tj** and **kj**:

tjock *thick*   tjugo *twenty*;   kjol *skirt*   Kjell (*man's name*)

C. Like "*soft*" *sk* ("show", "ach") are pronounced:

1. The combinations **sj, skj** and **stj**:

sju *seven*   sjuk *sick*   sjunga *sing*   sjö *lake*;   skjorta *shirt*;   stjäla *steal*
stjärna *star*

2. *Different consonants or consonant combinations* in loan-words which in the original language contain sounds similar to the "soft" sk-sound. The original spelling of the sound is preserved.

choklad *chocolate*   gara**ge** *garage*   **g**iraff *giraffe*   **j**ournalist *journalist*
stion *station*   musta**sch** *moustache*

2 **Further Notes on Consonants**

This letter is found mainly in foreign words. As a rule, it represents the same sound as in the corresponding word in English.

cigarr *cigar*   **c**ylinder   **c**ocktail   **c**amping   **ch**ampagne

Note 1. In the words "social" (*social*) "speciell" (*special*) *c* is pronounced like *s* in Swedish.

Note 2. The word "och" (*and*) as a separate word is pronounced as if it was spelled 'ock'. In connected speech, however, the word is usually reduced to "o". Cp. § 14.1.

d
t
n

d, *t* and *n* in Swedish are dental consonants, i.e. they are pronounced with the tip of the tongue against the upper teeth. In English they are pronounced further back: datum *date*   tant *aunt*   dansa *dance*

l

Similarly, *l* in Swedish is a dental consonant resembling *l* in British English 'lip', French 'lire'. The consonant is never pronounced as *ll* in English 'all': lampa *lamp*   glas *glass*   full *full*   hjälp *help*   kalk *lime*

ng

The combination *ng* is always pronounced like in English 'sing', never as in English 'finger'. It thus in Swedish represents one single sound.
lång *long*   finger *finger*   Ingrid   många *many*

gn

The combination *gn* is pronounced as if it was spelled *ng-n*.
regna *rain*   lugn *calm*   vagn *wagon*

r

Most Swedes pronounce *r* by faintly rolling the tip of the tongue.
ro *row*   brev *letter*   höra *hear*

rd
rl
rt
rn

In the combinations *rd*, *rl*, *rn*, *rt* the letter *r* is not pronounced. However, it influences the pronunciation of the following consonants so that these are pronounced almost like their English equivalents. Note the difference of pronunciation in the following word pairs:
mord *murder* — mod *courage*; farlig *dangerous* — salig *blessed*; sporta *go in for sports* — spotta *spit*; varna *warn* — vana *habit*

Note. *L* is mute in "värld" (*world*) and "karl" (*fellow, man*).

rs

This combination is pronounced with *one* sound resembling that of *sh* in English 'show': kors *cross*   person *person*

s

Swedish *s* is a dental consonant. It is always voiceless. Thus it is pronounced like *s* in English 'see' and never like in English 'easy'.
se *see*   is *ice*

x This consonant is pronounced like *cks*: exempel *example* läxa *lesson*

z This consonant is pronounced like *s*: zon *zone* zoologi *zoology*

Word Melody

13 English words with the stress on the first syllable have *one* general pattern of word melody when pronounced separately. It begins on one tone on the first syllable and then falls on the second syllable. (⌐➘).

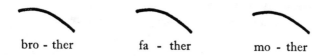

bro - ther   fa - ther   mo - ther

Swedish words have either of *two* kinds of word melody.

1. One is the *single-tone* melody which is similar to that of English words. In for instance the following words the word melody is similar in Swedish and English:*

Melody

Stress

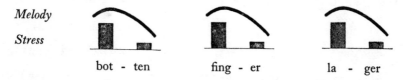

bot - ten   fing - er   la - ger

2. The second kind is the *double-tone* melody. In a word of two syllables with double tone the main stress is on the first syllable and the melody in that syllable is falling. The second syllable, however, gets a secondary stress and the melody rises to a new pitch on that syllable. The double-tone melody is used in most words of two or more syllables. The following words, for instance, have double tone:

Melody

Stress

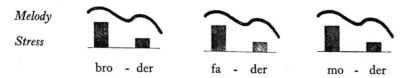

bro - der   fa - der   mo - der

---

* The Department of Phonetics, University of Stockholm, has been consulted about the illustrations.

These word melodies can be learned only by imitation.

Single-tone intonation is used in for instance

a) words of one syllable. Nouns of one syllable keep the single-tone intonation when the definite ending is added to them: park, parken *park, the park*   hus, huset   *house, the house*

b) present tense verb forms ending in -*er*: köper *buy, buys*   ställer *put, puts*

Double-tone intonation is used in for instance

a) most nouns of two syllables: gata *street*   nyckel *key*

b) verb forms ending in -*a, -ar, -ad, -ade, -at*: visa *show*   visar, visad, visade, visat

c) most compound words: landsväg *highway*   mörkblå *dark blue*

Colloquial Pronunciation

14 The written language and the spoken differ in various respects. Note the following forms of words that are found in the spoken language:

1. The final consonant is normally dropped in many common words:

   da|g *day*   de|t *it*   go|d *good*   ja|g *I*   me|d *with*   o|ch *and*   va|d *what*

2. Many pronouns have special colloquial forms: "mig, dig, sig" are pronounced "mej, dej, sej"; "de" and "dem" are often pronounced "dom"; "någon" and "sådan" are often contracted to "nån" and "sån".

3. Adjectives ending in -*ig* usually drop the *g* in the indefinite singular forms: vänli|g, vänli|g|t *friendly*

4. The past tense of the 1st conjugation of verbs often has the same form as the infinitive:

   att prata *to talk* — han prata' ("pratade" in the written language) *he talked*

   att titta *to look* — vi titta' ("tittade" in the written language) *we looked*

   The past tense forms of the verbs "säga" (*say*) and "lägga" (*put*) are usually written "sade" and "lade" but pronounced "sa" and "la".

Spelling

15   M and N

At the end of many common words of one syllable in which the vowel is *short*, *m* and *n* are not doubled in spelling. The vowel is short in for instance:

hem *home*   om *if*   rum *room*   vem *who*

den *it*   en *a, an, one*   han *he*   hon *she*   man *man*   vän *friend*

However, *between vowels m* and *n* are always doubled in spelling after short vowels. Thus *m* and *n* are doubled in the definite form of for instance the following words to indicate the short vowel: rum *room* — rummet *the room* man *man* — mannen *the man*   vän *friend* — vännen *the friend*.

A word containing a *double m* or *n* drops one *m* or *n* if another consonant is added after them in a declined form of the word:

nummer *number* — numret *the number*
sommar *summer* — somrar *summers*
sann *true* — sant *true* (neuter)
gammal *old* — gamla *old* (def. and plural)
glömma *forget* — glömde *forgot*
känna *know* — kände *knew*

Capitalization

16   Capital letters are used in about the same way in Swedish and English. Not capitalized in Swedish are, however:

1. names of days, months and festivals:
   söndag *Sunday*   september *September*   jul *Christmas*

2. nouns and adjectives denoting nationality, language, religion or party:
   en svensk *a Swede*;   en svensk bok *a Swedish book*;   han talar svenska *he speaks Swedish*;   han är protestant *he is a Protestant*;   han är social-demokrat *he is a Social Democrat*

3. titles used with names:
   herr Lundberg *Mr Lundberg*   fröken Lind *Miss Lind*
   doktor Persson *Doctor Persson*

NOUNS

Singular

En-Nouns and Ett-Nouns. Indefinite Form

17 Nouns in Swedish are of *two* kinds:

en bok *a book*	**ett** glas *a glass*

The nouns of one group take *the indefinite article "en"*. They can be called *en-nouns* (also called *non-neuter* nouns).

The nouns of the other group take *the indefinite article "ett"*. They can be called *ett-nouns* (also called *neuter* nouns).

18 *The group of en-nouns* is made up of nouns of masculine, feminine and common (en-nouns not denoting human beings) gender:

en man *a man*
en kvinna *a woman*
en bok *a book*

This is the larger group. Roughly speaking, 3/4 of the most common Swedish nouns are en-nouns.

Remarks on En-Nouns and Ett-Nouns

19 There is no general rule to fix what nouns are en-nouns and what are ett-nouns. To some extent, however, the *meaning* and the *form* of nouns indicate their gender.

En-Nouns Indicated by Meaning
Nouns denoting
a) *human beings:* en man *a man*   en kvinna *a woman*   en flicka *a girl*
b) *most animals:* en hund *a dog*   en katt *a cat*   en fågel *a bird*   en fisk *a fish*
c) *trees:* en björk *a birch*   en ek *an oak*   en gran *a spruce*   en alm *an elm-tree*
d) *seasons:* en höst *an autumn*   en sommar *a summer*   en vinter *a winter*
e) *festivals:* en jul *a Christmas*   en pingst *a Whitsuntide*   en påsk *an Easter*

Some Exceptions

a) ett barn *a child*   ett statsråd *a minister*
b) ett bi *a bee*   ett djur *an animal*   ett får *a sheep*   ett lejon *a lion*
c) ett träd *a tree*

En-Nouns Indicated by Form

Nouns ending in -*ad*, -*are*, -*dom*, -*het*, -*ing*, -*ion*, -*lek:*

    en månad *a month*   en målare *a painter*   en sjukdom *an illness*
    en nyhet *a piece of news*   en våning *an apartment, a flat*
    en diskussion *a discussion*   en storlek *a size*

Ett-Nouns Indicated by Meaning

Many nouns denoting *substances:*

    bröd *bread*   kaffe *coffee*   kött *meat*   papper *paper*
    salt *salt*   smör *butter*

Some Exceptions

    mjölk *milk*   olja *oil*   ost *cheese*   tobak *tobacco*

Ett-Nouns Indicated by Form

foreign nouns with the endings:

    -*ek:*   ett apotek *a chemist's*   ett bibliotek *a library*
    -*em:*   ett problem *a problem*   ett system *a system*
    -*iv:*   ett initiativ *an initiative*   ett motiv *a motive*
    -*um:*   ett museum *a museum*   ett observatorium *an observatory*

Definite Form

20

boken *the book*	glaset *the glass*

The definite article in Swedish is placed at the end of the noun.
The *definite article singular* for *en-nouns* is **-en**.
The *definite article singular* for *ett-nouns* is **-et**.

If a noun ends in a vowel, only **-n** or **-t** is added.

en blomm**a** *a flower*   blomma**n** *the flower*
ett äppl**e** *an apple*   äpple**t** *the apple*

Note. This does not apply to ett-nouns ending in a stressed vowel: ett bi ('a bee') biet ('the bee').

Some Rules about the Formation of the Singular Definite Form

21 For the doubling of *m* and *n* in the definite form of words like *rum, man* see § 15.

22 *En-nouns*

1. *En-nouns* ending in *unstressed -en* drop the *-e* before the definite ending:

   en säge**n** *a legend*   sägne**n** *the legend*
   en öke**n** *a desert*   ökne**n** *the desert*

2. Like en-nouns ending in a vowel, *en-nouns* ending in *unstressed -el* and *-er* add only *-n* in the definite singular (not *-en*):

   en nyck**el** *a key*   nyckel**n** *the key*
   en dott**er** *a daughter*   dotter**n** *the daughter*

3. The same rule applies to Latin words ending in *-or:*

   en dokt**or** *a doctor*   doktor**n** *the doctor*
   en profess**or** *a professor*   professor**n** *the professor*

23 *Ett-nouns*

1. *Ett-nouns* ending in unstressed *-el, -en, -er* drop the *-e* before the definite ending. Cp. § 26.1.

   ett exemp**el** *an example*   exemple**t** *the example*
   vatt**en** *water*   vattne**t** *the water*
   ett fönst**er** *a window*   fönstre**t** *the window*

2. Latin words ending in *-eum, -ium* drop the *-um* before the definite ending:

   ett mus**eum** *a museum*   muse**et** *the museum*
   ett observator**ium** *an observatory*   observatori**et** *the observatory*

Plural

Indefinite Form

24   There are five main ways of forming the plural of nouns in Swedish. These are *the five declensions*:

1.	en blomma	*a flower*	två blomm**or**	*two flowers*
2.	en arm	*an arm*	två arm**ar**	*two arms*
3.	en kostym	*a suit*	två kostym**er**	*two suits*
4.	ett äpple	*an apple*	två äppl**en**	*two apples*
5.	ett glas	*a glass*	två glas	*two glasses*

1st declension: plural ends in **-or**

The majority of nouns in this declension are *en-nouns ending in -a*. They drop the -a before the plural ending.

2nd declension: plural ends in **-ar**

All the nouns belonging to this declension are *en-nouns*.
(One exception: ett finger *a finger* två fing**rar** *two fingers*)

3rd declension: plural ends in **-er**

Both en-nouns and ett-nouns are found in this declension.
Note that many nouns in this group modify their stem-vowel in the plural; for a full list of these nouns see § 27.

4th declension: plural ends in **-n**

The majority of nouns in this declension are *ett-nouns ending in a vowel*, usually -e.

Note the change of final vowel in the plurals of:

ett öga *an eye*   två ög**on** *two eyes*
ett öra *an ear*   två ör**on** *two ears*

5th declension: no plural ending

To this declension belong e.g.

a) ett-nouns ending in a consonant

b) en-nouns ending in -are, -ande, and -ende:

en skomakare *a shoemaker*   två skomakare *two shoemakers*

en ordförande *a chairman*   två ordförande *two chairmen*

Note that some common nouns in this declension modify their stem-vowel:

en bro(de)r *a brother*   två bröder *two brothers*

en fa(de)r *a father*   två fäder *two fathers*

en man *a man*   två män *two men*

25 The following table shows the percentage of nouns in each declension in the 1000 most common Swedish words (from Allwood-Wilhelmsen: "Basic Swedish Word List").

1st decl.	en blomma	två blomm|or	12 %
2nd decl.	en arm	två arm|ar	37 %
3rd decl.	en kostym	två kostym|er	21 %
4th decl.	ett äpple	två äpple|n	4 %
5th decl.	ett glas	två glas	26 %
			100 %

26 Remarks about the Formation of the Plural Indefinite Form

1. Nouns ending in *unstressed -e, -el, -en, -er* drop the -e before the plural endings -or, -ar, -er. Cp. § 23.1.

1st declension

en toff**el** *a slipper*   två toff**lor** *two slippers*

en åd**er** *a vein*   två åd**ror** *two veins*

2nd declension

en pojk**e** *a boy*   två pojk**ar** *two boys*

en nyck**el** *a key*   två nyck**lar** *two keys*

en ök**en** *a desert*   två ök**nar** *two deserts*

en syst**er** *a sister*   två syst**rar** *two sisters*

With change of stem-vowel:

en dotter *a daughter*	två döttrar *two daughters*
en mo(de)r *a mother*	två mödrar *two mothers*

3rd declension

en regel *a rule*	två regler *two rules*
en sägen *a legend*	två sägner *two legends*
en neger *a negro*	två negrer *two negroes*

2. Note the following plurals in the second declension:

en afton *an evening*	två aftnar *two evenings*
en morgon *a morning*	två morgnar *two mornings*
en sommar *a summer*	två somrar *two summers*

(Regarding the dropping of one "m" in "somrar", see § 15.)

3. Some nouns form their plural with the ending *-r* only:

en händelse *an event*	två händelser *two events*

(Most nouns ending in *-else* form their plural in this way.)

en ko *a cow*	två kor *two cows*
en sko *a shoe*	två skor *two shoes*

With change of stem-vowel:

en bonde *a farmer*	två bönder *two farmers*

27 Added Comments on the Declensions

1st declension.

A few nouns in this group do not end in *-a:*

en ros *a rose*   en våg *a wave*   en åder *a vein*

2nd declension.

In this group are found all en-nouns ending in *-dom* and *-ing:*

en sjukdom *an illness*   en våning *a flat*

3rd declension. The following nouns modify their stem-vowel:

en and *a duck*	två änder *two ducks*
en brand *a fire*	två bränder *two fires*
en hand *a hand*	två händer *two hands*

ett land *a country*	två länder *two countries*
en rand *a stripe*	två ränder *two stripes*
en strand *a beach*	två stränder *two beaches*
en tand *a tooth*	två tänder *two teeth*
en stång *a pole*	två stänger *two poles*
en tång *a pair of tongs*	två tänger *two pairs of tongs*
en bokstav *a letter (in the alphabet)*	två bokstäver *two letters*
en ledamot *a member*	två ledamöter *two members*
en son *a son*	två söner *two sons*
en stad *a town*	två städer *two towns*
en natt *a night*	två nätter *two nights*

Some nouns modify their stem-vowel *and* double their final consonant in the plural:

en bok *a book*	två böcker *two books*
en fot *a foot*	två fötter *two feet*
en rot *a root*	två rötter *two roots*

Latin words ending in *-eum, -ium* belong to this declension.

They drop the *-um* before the plural ending:

ett mus**eum** *a museum*	två mus**eer** *two museums*
ett observator**ium** *an observatory*	två observator**ier** *two observatories*

Note the change of stress in the plural of nouns ending in *-or* in the third declension:

en d**o**ktor *a doctor*	två dokt**o**rer *two doctors*
en prof**e**ssor *a professor*	två profess**o**rer *two professors*
en tr**a**ktor *a tractor*	två trakt**o**rer *two tractors*

5th declension.

To this declension belong many en-nouns ending in *-er:*

en belgier *a Belgian*   en indier *an Indian*   en tekniker *a technician*
en musiker *a musician*

Singular and Plural: Indefinite and Definite Form

28 Definite Plural in -na.

DECL.	SINGULAR		PLURAL	
1st	en blomma blomman	*a flower* **the** *flower*	blommor blommorna	*flowers* **the** *flowers*
2nd	en arm armen	*an arm* **the** *arm*	armar armarna	*arms* **the** *arms*
3rd	en kostym kostymen	*a suit* **the** *suit*	kostymer kostymerna	*suits* **the** *suits*
5th	en bagare bagaren	*a baker* **the** *baker*	bagare bagarna	*bakers* **the** *bakers*
	en ordförande ordföranden	*a chairman* **the** *chairman*	ordförande ordförandena	*chairmen* **the** *chairmen*
	en belgier belgiern	*a Belgian* **the** *Belgian*	belgier belgierna	*Belgians* **the** *Belgians*

Most *en*-nouns take the *definite plural ending* **-na**.

Note. Nouns ending in *-are* drop the final -e before the definite plural ending.

29 Definite Plural in -a

DECL.	SINGULAR		PLURAL	
4th	ett äpple äpplet	*an apple* **the** *apple*	äpplen äpplena	*apples* **the** *apples*

Nouns of the fourth declension take the *definite plural ending* **-a**. Regarding "öga" and "öra" see below.

30 Definite Plural in -en

Decl.	Singular		Plural	
5th	ett glas	*a glass*	glas	*glasses*
	glas**et**	**the** *glass*	glas**en**	**the** *glasses*

Ett-nouns belonging to the fifth declension take the *definite plural ending -en.*

A few en-nouns take this plural ending, e.g.:

en man *a man* män *men*

mann**en** *the man* männ**en** *the men*

(Regarding the doubling of the *n* in "mannen, männen" see § 15.)

In this group are also:

ett öga *an eye* ögon *eyes*

öga**t** *the eye* ögon**en** *the eyes*

ett öra *an ear* öron *ears*

öra**t** *the ear* öron**en** *the ears*

31 Note. The ending *-en* can be:

1. the *singular definite* ending of en-nouns:

   arm**en** *the arm* bil**en** *the car*

2. the *plural definite* ending of nouns of the fifth declension:

   glas**en** *the glasses* männ**en** *the men*

3. the *plural indefinite* ending of nouns of the fourth declension:

   äppl**en** *apples* ställ**en** *places*

32 Remarks about the Formation of the Plural Definite Form

1. Ett-nouns ending in *unstressed -el, -en, -er* (*fifth declension*) drop the *-e* before the plural ending:

   ett exemp**el** *an example* exemp**len** *the examples*

   ett teck**en** *a sign* teck**nen** *the signs*

   ett fönst**er** *a window* fönst**ren** *the windows*

2. In the spoken language, the nouns of the fifth declension often have a definite plural form ending in -*a* in analogy with the rest of the nouns. Thus, in the spoken language, the following forms are heard:

glasena *the glasses*   exemplena *the examples*   fönstrena *the windows*

The spoken language definite plural forms of "ett öga", "ett öra" (*an eye, an ear*) are

ögona *the eyes*   örona *the ears*

Remarks on Number

33 Some words which are treated as *singular in English* are *plural in Swedish*, e.g.:

Har du sett våra nya *möbler*?	Have you seen our new *furniture*?
Har du *pengarna*? Nej, Karl har dem.	Do you have *the money*? No, Charles has *it*.
Kan ni ge mig några *upplysningar*?	Can you give me some *information*?

34 Some words are *plural in English* and *singular in Swedish*, e.g.:

Innehållet är utmärkt.	The *contents* are excellent.
Var är *saxen*?	Where are the *scissors*?
Var är *tången*?	Where are the *tongs*?

The Possessive Case

35 The possessive case is formed by adding -s to the noun, both in the indefinite and definite form, singular and plural.

Note that there is no apostrophe before -s in Swedish.

en kvinnas arbete	*a woman's* work
kvinnans arbete	*the woman's* work
kvinnors arbete	*women's* work
kvinnornas arbete	*the women's* work
en blommas färg	the colour *of a flower*
blommans färg	the colour *of the flower*
blommors färg	the colour *of flowers*
blommornas färg	the colour *of the flowers*

No extra -s is added to proper names ending in -s. In writing, an apostrophe is often added after the name:

Mats' bok *Mats's book*

The Use of the Possessive

36 The Swedish possessive can be used for inanimate objects and abstracts as well as for living beings. It thus corresponds to the English possessive in *'s* as well as to the English possessive with 'of':

pojkens båt	*the boy's* boat
pojkarnas båt	the boat *of the boys*
blommans färg	the colour *of the flower*
lampans storlek	the size *of the lamp*
sanningens röst	the voice *of Truth*

37 Note the use of the possessive in the following cases:

1. *Peter den stores* hov   the court *of Peter the Great*
   de fattigas tröst   the comfort *of the poor*
   Adjectives used as nouns can take the possessive -s.

2. Vi måste skriva till *Anderssons.*   We must write to *the Anderssons.*
   For names of families, where English uses the definite plural form, Swedish often uses the possessive.

3. en *trerums*våning   a *three-room* flat
   In Swedish compound nouns the first noun often takes a possessive -s (cp. § 40.2).

4. In set expressions with the prepositions "i" and "till" which formerly governed a following noun in the possessive case.
   "I" expresses past time in many common expressions of time. It is used particularly with days, seasons and festivals:

Han var här i söndags	*He was here last Sunday*
i måndags	*last Monday*
i tisdags	*last Tuesday*
etc.	*etc.*

i vintras	*last winter*
i våras	*last spring*
i somras	*last summer*
i höstas	*last autumn*
i julas	*last Christmas*
i påskas	*last Easter*

"Till" followed by a noun in the possessive is used in for instance the following expressions:

sitta till bords	*sit at table*
ligga till sängs	*be in bed*

See also § 270. D

Compound Nouns

38 A characteristic of Swedish is the frequency of compound nouns. Often Swedish joins the elements of a noun where English keeps them separate:

en bokhylla	*a book shelf*
en järnvägsstation	*a railway station*
en premiärminister	*a Prime Minister*

39 A compound noun takes the gender of the last element:

ett land + *en* väg = *en* landsväg (*a highway*)

40 Nouns can be joined in several ways:

1. The first element takes no ending:

en industri + ett land = ett industriland (*an industrial country*)
järn + en väg = en järnväg (*a railway*)
Sverige + ett besök = ett Sverigebesök (*a visit to Sweden*)

2. The first element takes a possessive -*s*:

ett land + en väg = en landsväg (*a highway*)
en bror + en dotter = en brorsdotter (*a niece*)
en järnväg + en station = en järnvägsstation (*a railway station*)
If the first element is a compound noun, this is the usual way of joining the elements.

3. An extra vowel is inserted between the nouns:

en familj + en försörjare = en familjeförsörjare (*a family supporter*)
en kung + ett rike = ett kungarike (*a kingdom*)

4. If the first element is a noun ending in -a, this vowel is sometimes changed into -*u* or -*o* (old possessive endings):

en vara + ett hus = ett varuhus (*a department store*)
en saga + en bok = en sagobok (*a book of fairy tales*)

5. The final vowel of the first noun is dropped:

en flicka + ett rum = ett flickrum (*a girl's room*)
en pojke + en vän = en pojkvän (*a boy friend*)

ADJECTIVES

The adjectives have an indefinite and a definite declension.

The Indefinite Declension

41

SINGULAR		
En-Words	*Ett-Words*	
en **stor** båt	ett **stort** glas	*a big boat (glass)*
båten är **stor**	glaset är **stort**	*the boat (glass) is big*
en **låg** hyra	ett **lågt** pris	*a low rent (price)*
hyran är **låg**	priset är **lågt**	*the rent (price) is low*

PLURAL		
två **stora** båtar	två **stora** glas	*two big boats (glasses)*
båtarna är **stora**	glasen är **stora**	*the boats (glasses) are big*
låga hyror	**låga** priser	*low rents (prices)*
hyrorna är **låga**	priserna är **låga**	*the rents (prices) are low*

Most adjectives have *two forms* in the *indefinite singular*:
1. the non-neuter form used with en-nouns (basic form): **stor, låg.**
2. the neuter form used with ett-nouns (basic form + t): **stort, lågt.**

All adjectives have *one form* for the *indefinite plural*, for en-nouns and ett-nouns alike (basic form + -a): **stora, låga.**

42 **Remarks on the Formation of the Neuter Form in the Indefinite Singular**

1. Adjectives ending in -d *preceded by a consonant* drop the -d before the t-ending:

En-Words	*Ett-Words*	
en *hård* vinter	ett *hårt* hjärta	*a hard winter (heart)*
vintern är *hård*	hjärtat är *hårt*	*the winter (heart) is hard*

33

2. Adjectives ending in *unstressed -en* drop the -n before the t-ending:

en *mogen* frukt	ett *moget* äpple	*a ripe fruit (apple)*
frukten är *mogen*	äpplet är *moget*	*the fruit (apple) is ripe*

3. Adjectives ending in a *stressed vowel* take *-tt* (not -t):

en *ny* bok	ett *nytt* hus	*a new book (house)*
boken är *ny*	huset är *nytt*	*the book (house) is new*

Note the change of pronunciation of the vowel. The vowel is *long* in "ny" and *short* in "nytt".

4. Adjectives ending in *-d preceded by a vowel* drop the -d and take *-tt*. Note the same change of pronunciation of the vowel as in 3.

en *röd* klänning	ett *rött* äpple	*a red dress (apple)*
klänningen är *röd*	äpplet är *rött*	*the dress (apple) is red*

Note that the same change of pronunciation is found in adjectives ending in *-t preceded by a long vowel:*

en *vit* blomma	ett *vitt* bord	*a white flower (table)*
blomman är *vit*	bordet är *vitt*	*the flower (table) is white*

5. Adjectives ending in *-t preceded by a consonant* remain unchanged in the neuter:

en *brant* backe	ett *brant* stup	*a steep hill (precipice)*
backen är *brant*	stupet är *brant*	*the hill (precipice) is steep*

Note that this applies to adjectives ending in *-tt:*

en *trött* man	ett *trött* barn	*a tired man (child)*
mannen är *trött*	barnet är *trött*	*the man (child) is tired*

6. Regarding adjectives ending in *-nn*, see § 15.

43 For remarks on the formation of the *indefinite plural form*, see the remarks below on the formation of the *definite form* of the adjective.

The Definite Declension

44

SINGULAR		
En-Words	*Ett-Words*	
den **stora** båten	det **stora** glaset	*the big boat (glass)*
den **låga** hyran	det **låga** priset	*the low rent (price)*

PLURAL		
de **stora** båtarna	*de* **stora** glasen	*the big boats (glasses)*
de **låga** hyrorna	*de* **låga** priserna	*the low rents (prices)*

The adjective has *only one form* in the *definite* declension, for both en-nouns and ett-nouns, for both singular and plural. This form is identical with the indefinite plural form (basic form + *a*): **stora, låga.**

45 Additional Definite Article

When an adjective precedes a noun in the definite form, there must be added, as a rule, an *additional definite article*. This is *"den"* for en-nouns and *"det"* for ett-nouns in the singular. In the plural, it is *"de"* for en-nouns and ett-nouns alike. (Originally, "den", "det" and "de" were demonstrative adjectives.)

Note that the noun always keeps its definite form: "den stora båt*en*, det stora glas*et*, de stora båtar*na*, de stora glas*en*".

For an illustration of the indefinite and definite declensions of the adjective in singular and plural see § 46.

46 Remarks on the Formation of the Indefinite Plural and the Definite Form of the Adjective

1. The indefinite plural form and the definite form of the adjective are identical. [One exception: "liten" ('small'), see below under 3.]

2. Adjectives ending in unstressed *-el, -en, -er* drop the *e* before the *a*-ending:

En-Words	*Ett-Words*	
en *enkel* fråga	ett *enkelt* problem	*a simple question (problem)*
enkla frågor	*enkla* problem	*simple questions (problems)*
den *enkla* frågan	det *enkla* problemet	*the simple question (problem)*
de *enkla* frågorna	de *enkla* problemen	*the simple questions (problems)*
en *förmögen* änka	ett *förmöget* hus	*a wealthy widow (house)*
förmögna änkor	*förmögna* hus	*wealthy widows (houses)*

den förmögna änkan	*det förmögna* huset	*the wealthy widow (house)*
de förmögna änkorna	*de förmögna* husen	*the wealthy widows (houses)*

en *vacker* flicka	ett *vackert* barn	*a pretty girl (child)*
vackra flickor	*vackra* barn	*pretty girls (children)*
den *vackra* flickan	det *vackra* barnet	*the pretty girl (child)*
de *vackra* flickorna	de *vackra* barnen	*the pretty girls (children)*

Note also the adjective "gammal" ('old'):

En-Words   *Ett-Words*

en *gammal* klocka	ett *gammalt* par	*an old clock (couple)*
gamla klockor	*gamla* par	*old clocks (couples)*
den *gamla* klockan	det *gamla* paret	*the old clock (couple)*
de *gamla* klockorna	de *gamla* paren	*the old clocks (couples)*

3. The adjective "liten" ('small') unlike other adjectives has a *separate plural form*. Its definite singular form is irregular:

en *liten* bil	ett *litet* kök	*a small car (kitchen)*
små bilar	*små* kök	*small cars (kitchens)*
den *lilla* bilen	det *lilla* köket	*the small car (kitchen)*
de *små* bilarna	de *små* köken	*the small cars (kitchens)*

4. When referring to males, the adjective in the definite singular sometimes ends in -*e* instead of -*a*. This is generally elevated style, but it is normal usage in
a) addressing men in letters: Kär**e** bror! *Dear brother!*
b) adjectives used as nouns: den avlidn**e** *the deceased* [*man*], Peter den stor**e** *Peter the Great*

47 Indeclinable Adjectives

A few adjectives have only one form which is used for en-nouns and ett-nouns in the singular and plural. These are the adjectives ending in -*a* and -*e*, e.g.:

en *bra* bok	ett *bra* ställe	*a good book (place)*
en *öde* ö	ett *öde* hus	*a desert island (house)*

Dropping of Additional Definite Article

48 Sometimes an adjective can precede a noun in the definite form without taking the additional definite article. This is the case in set expressions and names, e.g.: *Kungliga Slottet* The Royal Palace, *Vita huset* The White House, *Förenta Staterna* The United States.

Also before the ordinal numbers the additional definite article is often dropped:

Det var *första gången* han var här.	It was *the first time* he was here.
Han bor i *tredje huset* härifrån.	He lives in *the third house* from here.

Note. The additional definite article is also omitted before the adjectives "*hela*" ('the whole, all*/the/'), "*halva*" ('half /the/'), "*förra*" ('last'), and "*båda*" ('both /the/').

Hela familjen kom.	*The whole* (*all the*) *family* came.
Jag var där *förra året*.	It was there *last year*.
Halva huset brann ner.	*Half the house* burned down.
Båda pojkarna kan simma.	*Both boys* can swim.

If another adjective follows "hela", "halva", or "båda" the additional definite article is often inserted before the second adjective: "*hela |den| svenska nationen*" ('the whole Swedish nation'), "*halva |den| svenska befolkningen*" ('half the Swedish population'), "*båda |de| nya bilarna*" ('both |the| new cars').

* Concerning "hela" as a translation of the English 'all |the|', see § 143.

The Use of the Indefinite and the Definite Declensions of the Adjective

49 Adjectives can be used *attributively*, i.e. preceding a noun (en *stor* båt) or *predicatively*, i.e. following a verb (båten är *stor*).

The *predicative* adjective always takes the indefinite form. (For examples see §§ 41, 42.)

The *attributive* adjective sometimes takes the indefinite form and sometimes the definite form.

50 As a rule the **indefinite** form of the adjective is used together with the **indefinite** form of the noun.

SINGULAR		
En-Words	*Ett-Words*	
en ingen } **stor våning** vilken	ett inget } **stort rum** vilket	*a* *no* } *big flat (room)* *what a*
PLURAL		
två inga } **stora våningar** vilka	två inga } **stora rum** vilka	*two* *no* } *big flats (rooms)* *what*

Thus, the indefinite form of the adjective can be preceded by
a) the indefinite article, "en" or "ett"
b) numerals, "två, tre" etc.
c) an indefinite pronoun, e.g. "ingen"
d) an interrogative pronoun, e.g. "vilken"

51 Similarly, the **definite** form of the adjective is generally used together with the **definite** form of the noun.

SINGULAR den **stora våningen**	det **stora rummet**	*the big flat (room)*
PLURAL de **stora våningarna**	de **stora rummen**	*the big flats (rooms)*

The same construction is used after "den här, det här, de här" ('this, these') and "den där, det där, de där" ('that, those'): Den här *stora våningen*, det här *stora rummet* etc.

52 However, the **definite form of the adjective** is used together with the **indefinite form of the noun** after certain words.

SINGULAR		
En-Words	*Ett-Words*	
min Peters samma denna ⎬ **stora våning**	mitt Peters samma detta ⎬ **stora rum**	*my* *Peter's* *the same* *this* ⎬ *big flat (room)*
PLURAL		
mina Peters samma dessa ⎬ **stora våningar**	mina Peters samma dessa ⎬ **stora rum**	*my* *Peter's* *the same* *these* ⎬ *big flats (rooms)*

This is the case after the following words:

1. **Possessive words** (possessive adjectives, nouns in the possessive case, and the relative possessive pronoun "vars"):

hans *stora våning*   his big flat
flickans *röda klänning*   the girl's red dress
en man, *vars stora hus...*   a man whose big house...

Note, however, that the adjective "*egen*" ('own') usually takes the indefinite form after a possessive word: "*hans egen våning*" ('his own flat') "*deras eget fel*" ('their own fault').

2. **The determinatives "den — som, det — som, de — som":**
det *stora rum* som ...   the big room that ...

3. **The adjectives "följande"** ('*the following*'), **"nästa"** ('*the next*'), **and "samma"** ('*the same*'):
följande *goda idé*   the following good idea
nästa *gula hus*   the next yellow house
samma *röda klänning*   the same red dress

4. The demonstrative adjective "denna, detta, dessa":

denna *goda idé*   this good idea

dessa *vackra träd*   these beautiful trees

Note the different construction after "den här, det där" etc. mentioned above in § 51.

53 The following is a table of the use of the forms of the adjective and noun after certain words.

I = indefinite form. D = definite form

QUALIFIER	ADJEC-TIVE	NOUN
en, ett (indefinite article)	I	I
två, tre, etc. (numerals)	I	I
vilken, vilket, vilka ('which', 'what')	I	I
ingen, inget, inga ('no')	I	I
någon, något, några ('any, some')	I	I
varje ('every, each')	I	I
flera ('several'), många ('many')	I	I
den, det, de (definite article or demonstrative adjective)	D	D
den här, det här ('this'), de här ('these')	D	D
den där, det där ('that'), de där ('those')	D	D
All possessive adjectives, nouns in the possessive case	D	I
den (... som), det (... som), de (... som) (i.e. the determinative adjective)	D	I
samma ('the same')	D	I
nästa ('next', 'the next')	D	I
följande ('the following')	D	I
föregående ('the previous')	D	I
denna, detta ('this'), dessa ('these')	D	I

Note. The word "fel" ('the wrong') is used together with the indefinite form of the noun: "fel tåg" ('the wrong train'). This is often the case also with "rätt" ('the right'): "rätt person [den rätta personen]" ('the right person').

Comparison of Adjectives

54

Positive	Comparative	Superlative
kall *cold* billig *cheap*	kall**are** *colder* billig**are** *cheaper*	kall**ast** *coldest* billig**ast** *cheapest*

Most Swedish adjectives are compared like "kall" and "billig", adding the endings *-are* in the comparative and *-ast* in the superlative.

An adjective ending in unstressed *-el*, *-en*, *-er* in the positive drops the -e of the ending before the comparative and superlative endings.

en**kel** *simple*	en**klare**	en**klast**
mo**gen** *ripe*	mo**gnare**	mo**gnast**
vac**ker** *pretty*	vac**krare**	vac**krast**

55 A few adjectives take the endings *-re* in the comparative and *-st* in the superlative. In addition all of them, except "hög", modify their stem-vowel.

Positive	Comparative	Superlative
hög *high*	högre	högst
grov *coarse*	grövre	grövst
stor *big*	större	störst
tung *heavy*	tyngre	tyngst
ung *young*	yngre	yngst
låg *low*	lägre	lägst
lång *long*	längre	längst
trång *narrow*	trängre	trängst
få *few*	färre	—

56 A few adjectives have comparative and superlative forms which are made from stems other than the positive.

Positive	Comparative	Superlative
dålig *bad, poor*	sämre	sämst
dålig, ond *bad, evil*	värre	värst

gammal *old*	äldre	äldst
god [bra] *good*	bättre	bäst
liten *little, small*	mindre	minst
många *many*	fler(a)	de flesta

57 The Comparative

The comparative has only *one* form, which is used for en-nouns and ett-nouns in the singular and plural, definite and indefinite.

en *billigare* bok	a cheaper book
ett *billigare* hus	a cheaper house
billigare böcker (hus)	cheaper books (houses)
den *billigare* boken	the cheaper book
det *billigare* huset	the cheaper house
de *billigare* böckerna (husen)	the cheaper books (houses)

58 The Superlative

The superlative of every adjective has *two* forms, an indefinite and a definite form.

1. *Indefinite form*

This is the basic form ending in -*ast* or -*st*. It is used for en-nouns and ett-nouns in the singular and plural.

Var är vintern *kallast*?	Where is the winter coldest?
Var är vattnet *kallast*?	Where is the water coldest?
Var är vintrarna *kallast*?	Where are the winters coldest?
Var är svårigheten *störst*?	Where is the difficulty greatest?
Var är problemet *störst*?	Where is the problem greatest?
Var är svårigheterna (problemen) *störst*?	Where are the difficulties (problems) greatest?

2. *Definite form*

For most adjectives this is the basic form + -*e* and for some the basic form + -*a*. The same form is used for en-nouns and ett-nouns in the singular and plural.

a) Superlatives ending in -*ast* take the ending -*e* in the definite form:

den *kall*aste vintern   the coldest winter
det *kall*aste vädret   the coldest weather
de *kall*aste vintrarna   the coldest winters

b) Superlatives ending in -*st* take the ending -*a* in the definite form:

den *stör*sta svårigheten   the greatest difficulty
det *stör*sta problemet   the greatest problem
de *stör*sta svårigheterna (pro-   the greatest difficulties (problems)
blemen)

59 The Use of the Indefinite and the Definite Form of the Superlative

The *indefinite form* is used predicatively, after verbs like "vara, bliva". The use of the indefinite form is the same in English and Swedish.

Gräset är *grönast* på våren.   The grass is *greenest* in the spring.
Det ska bli *kallast* i norra Sverige.   It will be *coldest* in northern Sweden.

The *definite form* is used in the same way as the definite form of the adjective in the positive. (See § 51, 52.)

Note 1. The definite form of the superlative can be used predicatively after verbs like "vara, bliva". It is then preceded by the additional definite article "den", "det" or "de". The superlative is then in the definite form also in English:

Den här boken *är den billigaste*.   This book *is the cheapest*.
Det här huset *är det billigaste*.   This house *is the cheapest*.

Note 2. In some prepositional phrases the definite form of the superlative is used together with the indefinite form of the noun. Note, too, that the additional definite article is omitted:

         i bästa fall   in the best case, at best
         i första hand   in the first place
         i högsta grad   to the highest degree, highly
         i minsta detalj   in the smallest detail
         i sista hand   in the last resort

60 Comparison with "mer(a)" and "mest"

The comparative and superlative forms of some adjectives are made
by placing the words "*mer(a), mest*" ('more, most') before the adjectives and not by means of endings. This applies to the adjectives ending
in -*isk* and to all *participles* used as adjectives.

en *typisk* svensk	a typical Swede
en *mer typisk* svensk	a more typical Swede
den mest typiske svensken	the most typical Swede
en *intresserad* lyssnare	an interested listener
en *mer intresserad* lyssnare	a more interested listener
den mest intresserade lyssnaren	the most interested listener

61 The Comparative Used in an Absolute Sense

In Swedish, the comparative is often used in an absolute sense. In translation the comparative can often best be rendered by the adjective in the
positive in English.

ett mindre samhälle	a small community
en större summa pengar	a large sum of money
en äldre herre	an elderly gentleman

62 Adjectives Used as Nouns

Adjectives (and participles) are more commonly used as nouns in Swedish
than in English.

Ska jag ta den gröna eller den röda slipsen? — Ta *den röda.*	Shall I take the green or the red tie? — Take *the red one.*
Den försvunne var klädd i svart överrock.	*The man who has disappeared* was dressed in a black overcoat.

Thus in examples like the first the word 'one' is not translated into Swedish. Cp. § 300.2 b.

NUMERALS

CARDINAL NUMBERS

ORDINAL NUMBERS

	CARDINAL	ORDINAL
0	noll	
1	en, ett	första
2	två	andra
3	tre	tredje
4	fyra	fjärde
5	fem	femte
6	sex	sjätte
7	sju	sjunde
8	åtta	åttonde
9	nio	nionde
10	tio	tionde
11	elva	elfte
12	tolv	tolfte
13	tretton	trettonde
14	fjorton	fjortonde
15	femton	femtonde
16	sexton	sextonde
17	sjutton	sjuttonde
18	arton *or* aderton	artonde *or* adertonde
19	nitton	nittonde
20	tjugo	tjugonde
21	tjugoen (-ett)	tjugoförsta
22	tjugotvå	tjugoandra
	etc.	
30	trettio	trettionde
40	fyrtio	fyrtionde
50	femtio	femtionde
60	sextio	sextionde
70	sjuttio	sjuttionde

CARDINAL NUMBERS	ORDINAL NUMBERS
80 åttio	åttionde
90 nittio	nittionde
100 (ett)hundra	hundrade
101 (ett)hundraen (-ett)	(ett)hundraförsta
1000 (ett)tusen	tusende
1001 (ett)tusenen (-ett)	(ett)tusenförsta
2000 tvåtusen	tvåtusende

1,000,000 en miljon
3,500,000 tre miljoner femhundra tusen
1,000,000,000 en miljard
2,000,000,000 två miljarder
1,000,000,000,000 en biljon (en miljon miljoner)

Note 1. "Tjugoen, tjugotvå," etc. are often pronounced "tjuen, tjutvå" etc.

Note 2. "Trettio, fyrtio" etc. are often pronounced "tretti, fyrti" etc.

Note 3. "En biljon" is not the American "one billion", but "one trillion".

Some Expressions with Numerals

64 Dates

Han är född *1935* (nittonhundra-trettiofem).	He was born *in 1935.*
Han är född *den 17* (sjuttonde) *mars 1935.*	He was born *on the seventeenth of March, 1935.*
Brevet är daterat:	The letter is dated:
Stockholm *den 6 juni 1809* (arton-hundranio).	Stockholm, *June 6, 1809.*

Note. The prepositions "in" before years and "on" before dates in English have no equivalents in Swedish.

Den industriella revolutionen började i England *på 1700-talet.*	The industrial revolution started in England *in the 18th century.*
Charleston var modernt *på tjugotalet.*	The Charleston was popular *in the twenties.*

Note. "På 1800-talet" = in the 19th century
"På 1900-talet" = in the 20th century
etc.
"På nittonhundratjugotalet" = in the nineteen-twenties
"På trettiotalet" = in the thirties
etc.

5 The Time

Möt mig *klockan fem.*	Meet me *at five o'clock.*
(*en*) *kvart över fem.*	*at a quarter past five.*
halv sex.	*at half past five.*
(*en*) *kvart i sex.*	*at a quarter to six.*

Note. The preposition "at" before hours has no equivalent in Swedish.

6 The Numerals as Nouns

Ta *åttan* eller *sexan* till Slussen.	Take tram *number eight* or *six* to Slussen.
Jag vet inte om det är *en etta* eller *en sjua.*	I don't know whether it is *a one* or *a seven.*

The numerals 1–12 can be made into nouns by adding *-a:* "en etta, tvåa, trea", etc. These nouns belong to the first declension and thus take the plural ending *-or.* The figure 0 as a noun is "en nolla", also of the first declension.

7 Fractional Numbers

1/2 = en halv;   1/3 = en tredjedel;   1/4 = en fjärdedel;   1/8 = en åttondel;   3/5 = tre femtedelar

Fractional numbers are formed by adding *-del* (plural *-delar*) to the ordinal number. The *de-*ending of the ordinal number is dropped except in "fjärdedel, sjundedel".

3 1/2 (*tre och ett halvt*) *kilo* potatis	*Three and a half kilos* of potatoes
1/4 (*ett kvarts*) *kilo smör*	*A quarter of a kilo* of butter
Vi väntade *en kvart*.	We waited for *a quarter of an hour*.

68   Some Collective Numbers

Ett par dagar	*A couple of* days
Ett dussin pennor	*A dozen of* pencils
Ett tjog ägg	*A score of* eggs

Note. The preposition 'of' has no equivalent in Swedish after words denoting quantity. Cp. § 280.1.

PRONOUNS

Personal Pronouns

59 In Swedish as in English, most personal pronouns have one form (subject form) when used as subjects, and another one (object form) when used as objects or governed by a preposition.

Number	Person	Subj. form	Obj. form
Sing.	1	jag *I*	mig *me*
	2	du *you*	dig *you*
		ni *you*	er *you*
	3	han *he*	honom *him*
		hon *she*	henne *her*
		den *it*	den *it*
		det *it*	det *it*
Plur.	1	vi *we*	oss *us*
	2	ni *you*	er *you*
	3	de *they*	dem *them*

Note 1. In formal style "er" is sometimes replaced by the older form "eder".

Note 2. In English the subject and object forms of 'you' are identical. In Swedish there are two separate forms.

Du/Ni måste ge oss pengarna.   *You* must give us the money.

Vi måste ge *dig/er* pengarna.   We must give *you* the money.

Terms of Address

70 The two 2nd person pronouns in the singular both correspond to 'you', but there is an important difference between them.

You use "du, dig" speaking to relatives, intimate friends, school friends, children, etc. (i.e., generally speaking, to people whom you address by their first names). Adults usually do not address each other by "du, dig" until they have formally agreed to do so ("dropped their titles"). However, members of a "group" (students at a school, employees of a firm, etc.) often say "du" to one another without individual agreements.

"Ni, er" is used when you speak to somebody you do not know very well (cp. "vous" in French). In such cases it would be impolite to use "du, dig". If you know the name of a person whom you are not supposed to address by "du, dig", the name preceded by a title (or the title in the definite form) is considered more polite as a form of address than "ni, er". When you do not know the name of the person you speak to you may replace "ni, er" by "min herre" (to a man) or "damen" (to a lady).

In the plural "ni, er" is the only pronoun of the 2nd person. Speaking to two or several people whom you do not address by "du, dig" you sometimes use expressions such as "herrarna" (*the gentlemen*) or "damerna" (*the ladies*) to replace "ni, er".

Hör *du* mig, Gustav?	Do *you* hear me, Gustav?
Har *ni* en tändsticka? Har *min herre* en tändsticka?	Have *you* got a match, *sir*?
Väntar *ni* på någon? Väntar *damen* på någon?	Are *you* waiting for somebody, *Madam?*
Var bor *ni, herr Larsson?* Var bor *herr Larsson?*	Where do *you* live, *Mr. Larsson?*
Har *ni* träffat min man, *fru West-lund?* Har *fru Westlund* träffat min man?	Have *you* met my husband, *Mrs. Westlund?*
Får jag ringa *er* i morgon, *fröken Ström?* Får jag ringa *fröken Ström* i morgon?	May I call *you* up to-morrow, *Miss Ström?*

Kommer *ni* ihåg mig, *doktor Hell-*
man?

Kommer *doktor Hellman* ihåg

mig?

Kommer *doktorn* ihåg mig?

}

Do *you* remember me, *doctor*
Hellman?

Vad önskar *ni, mina herrar?*

Vad önskar *herrarna?*

}

What do *you* want, *gentlemen?*

The following simplified survey may prove helpful.

SITUATION	TRANSLATION OF 'YOU'			
	SINGULAR		PLURAL	
	SUBJECT	OBJECT	SUBJECT	OBJECT
A. Speaking to people whom you address by their first names.	du	dig	ni	er
B. Speaking to people whom you do not know.	ni *or* min herre *or* damen	er *or* min herre *or* damen	ni *or* herrarna *or* damerna	er *or* herrarna *or* damerna
C. Speaking to people whose names and/ or titles you know but whom you are not supposed to address by their first names.	ni *or* herr A. (fru A., frö- ken A.) *or* doktor A. *or* doktorn	er *or* herr A. (fru A., frö- ken A.) *or* doktor A. *or* doktorn	ni *or* herrarna *or* damerna	er *or* herrarna *or* damerna

Use of "den" and "det"

71 As for the two words corresponding to 'it' the general rule is that
"den" refers to non-neuter nouns, "det" to neuter nouns.

Var är ring*en*? — Jag har *den* här.	Where is the ring? — I have it here.
Vilken färg har tak*et*? — *Det* är vitt.	What colour is the ceiling? — It is white.

Use of "det"

However, the neuter form "det" is also used in many other cases and does not always correspond to 'it' in English. The most important cases where "det" is used are the following:

72 "Det" Corresponding to English 'It'

1. "Det" refers back to a neuter noun. See above § 71.

2. "Det" is used without specific reference (unlike "den" which always refers to a noun). This is the case:

   a) in impersonal expressions.

Det regnar.	*It is raining.*
Det är kallt ute.	*It is cold* outside.

   b) when "det" is the subject of some form of "vara" or "bli" ('be') *followed by a noun* (sometimes called predicative noun).

Är det en tiger? — Nej, *det är ett lejon.*	*Is it a tiger?* — No, *it is a lion.*
Vi trodde, att *det var en komet.*	We thought that *it was a comet.*
Lyssnar du på föreläsningen? — Ja, *det är en intressant föreläsning.*	Are you listening to the lecture? — Yes, *it is an interesting lecture.*

Note 1. If there is no noun but only a predicative adjective after 'it is ...' etc. you apply the general rule for the use of "den" and "det": "Lyssnar du på *föreläsningen*?" — "Ja, *den är intressant.*" ('— Yes, *it is interesting.*')

Note 2. The same rule applies to the use of "detta", "det här", and "det där" as equivalents of 'this' or 'that' (cp. below demonstrative pronouns), i.e. neuter forms are used when the pronoun is followed by "vara" or "bli" + predicative noun.

Det här är en runsten.   *This* is a rune-stone.

Translation of 'it'

73 The rules for the translation of 'it' into Swedish could be summarized (in a somewhat simplified form) thus:

1. If *'it' refers to a noun* you use "den" when the Swedish noun is non-neuter, "det" when the noun is neuter.

2. When you have the construction *'it'* + *some form of 'be'* + *a noun* you use "det", even if 'it' in English may seem to refer to a non-neuter noun.

3. In *other cases*, i.e. when it is clear that 'it' does not refer to any particular noun, "det" should be used in Swedish.

74 **"Det" Not Corresponding to English 'It'**

1. "Det" is often used to translate the English 'he', 'she', or 'they' in the expressions 'he is', 'she is', 'they are' + a noun (cp. § 72.2 b above).

Vem är den där damen? —   Who is that lady? — *She is* my
Det är min svärmor.   mother-in-law.

2. "Det" is used to translate the English 'there' in the different Swedish equivalents of the expressions 'there is', 'there are', 'there was', 'there were', etc.

Det är många besökare här   *There are* many visitors here to-
idag.   day.
Det var en gång en liten pojke... Once *there was* a little boy ...
Det finns inte ett enda hotell i   *There is* not a single hotel in this
den här staden.   town.

3. "Det" is used to translate the English 'so' as an object of certain verbs, especially those meaning 'think', 'hope', 'suppose'.

Jag *tror* (*hoppas, antar*) *det.*   I *think* (*hope, suppose*) *so.*

4. "Det", together with "också" (also), is used corresponding to English 'so' when 'so' means 'also'.

Barnen är hungriga, och *det* är   The children are hungry and *so*
jag *också.*   am I.

5. "Det" is used without an English equivalent together with forms of "vara, bli" and as an object of certain other verbs, particularly the auxiliaries and the verbs meaning 'do' and 'tell'. In these cases "det" usually starts the clause.

Är du trött? — Ja, *det är* jag.   Are you tired? — Yes, *I am.*

Kan han simma? — Ja, *det kan*   Can he swim? — Yes, *he can.*
han.

Känner ni fröken A.? — Nej,   Do you know Miss A.? — No,
det gör jag inte.   *I don't.*

Det talade han inte om för mig.   He didn't *tell* me.

Reflexive Pronouns

75	NUMBER	PERSON	
	SINGULAR	1	mig *myself*
		2	dig *yourself* er *yourself*
		3	sig *himself, herself, itself, oneself*
	PLURAL	1	oss *ourselves*
		2	er *yourselves*
		3	sig *themselves*

76 The reflexive pronouns are identical with the object forms of the personal pronouns, except for the 3rd person which has a special reflexive form "sig", used both in the singular and plural. The term "reflexive" refers to the fact that these pronouns represent ("refer back to") the subject of the clause in which they occur.

Vi *roade oss.*	We *enjoyed ourselves.*
Jag försöker *lära mig* ryska.	I am trying to *learn (literally: teach myself)* Russian.
Slog du *dig?* *Slog* ni *er?*	Did you *hurt yourself?*
Han *skar sig.*	He *cut himself.*
Hon har *solat sig* hela dagen.	She has been *sunning herself* all day.
De *kastade sig* in i striden.	They *threw themselves* into the fight.
Det är nödvändigt att kunna *försvara sig.*	It is necessary to be able to *defend oneself.*

Note. "Sig" also corresponds to English 'him', 'her', 'it', 'them' when these words have a reflexive meaning in English. This often occurs when they are the object of a preposition.

Han tittade framför *sig.*	He looked in front of *him.*
De lämnade två barn efter *sig.*	They left two children behind *them.*

77 A verb combined with a reflexive pronoun is called a reflexive verb. For comments on reflexive verbs see § 222.

Emphatic Pronouns

78 The English reflexive pronouns are also used as emphatic pronouns, i.e. to give emphasis to a noun or pronoun already mentioned. In Swedish there is a special emphatic pronoun "*själv*" to translate 'myself', 'yourself', 'himself', 'herself', 'itself' and 'oneself' with a plural form *"själva"* to translate 'ourselves', 'yourselves', and 'themselves'.

Har *du* skrivit den här uppsatsen *själv?*	Have *you* written this paper *yourself?*
Statsministern själv ska öppna utställningen.	The Prime Minister *himself* is to open the exhibition.
Vi vet ganska mycket om landet, fastän *vi* inte har varit där *själva*.	We know a good deal about the country although *we* have not been there *ourselves*.

Note. *"Själv"* may take on a special neuter form, *"självt"*, but the basic form (without t-ending) is also commonly used in the neuter.

Det säger sig *själv(t)*.	It goes without saying.

79 Distinction between Reflexive and Emphatic Pronouns

As implied above, the English pronouns 'myself', 'yourself', etc. may be translated into Swedish in two different ways: if they have a reflexive meaning you use "mig", "dig", "sig", etc.; if they have an emphatic meaning you use "själv (-t, -a)". To find out the correct translation in a particular case, try to remove the pronoun concerned in English. If it can be removed without changing the basic meaning of the sentence, it is usually an emphatic pronoun which should be translated by "själv (-t, -a)"; if not, you use the reflexive pronouns. Examples, see above §§ 76 and 78.

Note. 'Myself', 'yourself', etc. in English may be reflexive and emphatic at the same time. In such cases a reflexive as well as an emphatic pronoun is used in Swedish. This construction also occurs when the subject of a reflexive verb is emphasized by "själv (-t, -a)".

"Vad ska jag göra?" sade han för *sig själv*.	"What shall I do?", he said to *himself*.
Den här gången har du överträffat *dig själv*.	This time you have surpassed *yourself*.

Possessive Pronouns and Adjectives

80 Possessive adjectives and possessive pronouns have common forms in Swedish: "min" corresponds to both 'my' and 'mine', "din" both to 'your' and to 'yours' etc. Below, the term "possessive pronoun" is used as a common term for both these types of pronominal words.

81 The following table presents the basic forms of the possessive pronouns in Swedish.

NUMBER	PERSON			
SINGULAR	1	min	*my, mine*	
	2	din er	*your, yours*	
	3	hans hennes dess	*his,* *her, hers* *its*	non-reflexive
		sin	*his, her* *hers, its*	reflexive
PLURAL	1	vår	*our, ours*	
	2	er	*your, yours*	
	3	deras	*their, theirs*	non-reflexive
		sin	*their, theirs*	reflexive

82 "Din" and "er" in the singular are the possessive equivalents of the personal pronouns "du, dig" and "ni, er" i.e. you use "din" when speaking to a person you address by "du, dig" and "er" to a person you address by "ni, er". When you address a person by title or title + name, the possessive form of this title or name can be used as the equivalent of 'your, yours'.

Här är *din* hatt, Gustav.　　　　Here is *your* hat, Gustav.

Här är *er* hatt.

Här är *min herres* hatt.　　　　Here is *your* hat, sir.

Här är *er* hatt, doktor Hellman. ⎫
Här är *doktor Hellmans* hatt. ⎬ Here is *your* hat, doctor Hellman.
Här är *doktorns* hatt. ⎭

83 The word "sin" is reflexive, i.e. it refers to the subject of the clause in which it occurs. English 'his', 'her', 'its', 'their' must be rendered by "sin" when the following *two* conditions are both present in a clause:

1. The possessive word qualifies the object in the clause (direct object or object of a preposition)

   and

2. the owner is the subject of the clause.

In all other cases, English 'his', 'her', 'its', 'their' must be rendered by "hans", "hennes", "dess", "deras".

Han lagade *sin bil.*	He repaired *his (own) car.*
Han lagade *hans bil.*	He repaired *his (another person's) car.*
Hon skriver ett brev till *sin man.*	She is writing a letter to *her (own) husband.*
Hon skriver ett brev till *hennes man.*	She is writing a letter to *her (another person's) husband.*
Partiet har förlorat *sin ledare.*	The party has lost *its leader.*
Partiet är ganska litet, men *dess ledare* är en skicklig politiker.	The party is quite small but *its leader* is a clever politician.
Herr och fru Olsson ska hälsa på *sin son.*	Mr. and Mrs. Olsson are going to visit *their (own) son.*
Vi har aldrig träffat *deras son.*	We have never met *their son.*
Du måste be *hennes föräldrar* om ursäkt.	You must apologize to *her parents.*
Mästaren försvarade *sin titel.*	The champion defended *his title.*

Note. "Sin" can never be used to qualify the subject of a clause. In the first of the following examples there are two subjects; 'his' is placed before the second subject and must thus be translated by "hans".

Direktören och *hans sekreterare* har rest utomlands.

The director and *his secretary* have gone abroad.

but

Direktören har rest utomlands med *sin sekreterare.*

The director has gone abroad with *his (own) secretary.*

84 "Hans", "hennes", "dess" and "deras" are indeclinable. The other possessive pronouns are declined to agree with the word they qualify (like adjectives in the indefinite form). The following are the forms of inflection:

Number and gender of the word qualified

SINGULAR		PLURAL
Non-neuter	*Neuter*	*(both genders)*
min	mitt	mina
din	ditt	dina
sin	sitt	sina
vår	vårt	våra
er	ert	era

Min plånbok är tom.
Mitt glas är tomt.
Mina fickor är tomma.

My wallet is empty.
My glass is empty.
My pockets are empty. .

Han älskar *sin hustru.*
Han älskar *sitt arbete.*
Han älskar *sina barn.*

He loves *his wife.*
He loves *his work.*
He loves *his children.*

Våningen är *vår*.	*The flat* is *ours*.
Landet är *vårt*.	*The country* is *ours*.
Böckerna är *våra*.	*The books* are *ours*.
Hans bil är stor.	*His car* is big.
Hans hus är stort.	*His house* is big.
Hans fötter är stora.	*His feet* are big.

85 In formal style "er, ert, era" are sometimes replaced by the older forms "eder, edert, edra".

86 Note that English 'her' has three Swedish equivalents:

1. "henne" when 'her' is the object form of the personal pronoun: "Jag känner *henne*." (*I know her*.);

2. "hennes" when 'her' is a possessive adjective with non-reflexive meaning: Jag känner *hennes* bror." (*I know her brother*.);

3. "Sin, sitt, sina", when 'her' is a possessive adjective with reflexive meaning: "Hon älskar *sin* man." (*She loves her husband*.).

87 English possessive adjectives qualifying parts of the body, clothing, etc. are often rendered by the definite article in Swedish (as in French and German).

Sätt på dig överrock*en*!	Put on *your* overcoat!
Hon räckte mig hand*en*.	She gave me *her* hand.

Relative Pronouns

Som, vilken

88 The two most common relative pronouns in Swedish are "*som*" and "*vilken*" both of which are used as equivalents of 'who(m)', 'which', 'that' or 'as'. "Som" is inflexible. The following is the inflexion of "vilken":

vilken (referring to non-neuter)
vilket ("   " neuter)
vilka ("   " plural)

9 "Som" is by far the most commonly used of the two pronouns. On the whole, "vilken (vilket, vilka)" should be used instead of "som" only in those cases where "som" would be incorrect grammatically (see below §§ 90, 91).

Jag har en farbror, *som* bor i Köpenhamn.	I have an uncle *who* lives in Copenhagen.
De erbjöd oss ett bord, *som* såg mycket trevligt ut.	They offered us a table *which* looked very nice.
Det här är boken, *som* han gav mig.	This is the book *that* he gave me.

0 "Som" cannot be preceded by a preposition. In clauses where a relative pronoun is governed by a preposition two constructions are possible:

1. The clause starts with "som" and the preposition is placed at the end of the clause.

2. The clause starts with the preposition followed by "vilken (vilket, vilka)".

Staden, *som* de flyttade *till* ... ⎫
Staden, *till vilken* de flyttade... ⎬ The city *to which* they moved ...
                                     ⎭

In conversation the first construction is by far the most common.

1 When the relative pronoun refers to a whole clause (not to a special word) "som" cannot be used. In such cases the neuter form "vilket" is the usual equivalent of English 'which'.

De lovade att snart komma tillbaka, vilket gjorde honom mycket glad.	*They promised to come back soon which* made him very happy.

Vars

2 In the possessive case there is a special pronoun "*vars*" which corresponds to 'whose' or 'of which' in English. "Vars" is used only to refer to a noun

in the singular. In the plural the possessive form of "vilka", *"vilkas"*, is used.

Mannen, vars ansikte föreföll mig bekant, visade sig vara en berömd författare.	*The man whose face* appeared well-known to me, turned out to be a famous author.
De båda männen, vilkas identitet man först var osäker om, visade sig vara två arbetare från trakten.	*The two men whose identity* was uncertain at first turned out to be two workmen from the neighbourhood.
Detta är *ett påstående, vars giltighet* jag ifrågasätter.	This is *a statement the validity of which* I question.

In the singular there are also the possessive forms "vilkens, vilkets" but these are rarely used.

Vad

93 *"Vad"* is sometimes used as a relative pronoun corresponding to 'that' or 'what' in English.

Detta är *allt, vad* jag har hört om det.	This is *all that* I have heard about it.
Jag ska göra *vad* jag kan.	I shall do *what* I can.

94 As in English, the relative pronoun is often left out (only implied by the context). Normally this may be done in all cases where it would be possible in English.

Skorna, (som) jag köpte, var mycket dyra.	*The shoes I bought* were very expensive.

Demonstrative Pronouns and Adjectives

95 The principal demonstrative pronouns are *"denna"* ('this'), *"den här"* ('this'), *"den"* ('that'), and *"den där"* ('that'). These words are also used as demonstrative adjectives. The forms are:

Non-neuter	*Neuter*	*Plural*
denna *this*	detta *this*	dessa *these*
den här *this*	det här *this*	de här *these*
den *that*	det *that*	de *those*
den där *that*	det där *that*	de där *those*

6 When these words are used as demonstrative adjectives (i.e. when they are followed by a noun) the following noun takes the *indefinite form* after *"denna (detta, dessa)"* but the *definite form after the others*. A form "denne" is sometimes used instead of "denna" qualifying or referring to a noun of masculine gender.

Denna man är min vän.	
Denne man är min vän.	*This man* is my friend.
Den här mannen är min vän.	
Detta väder gör mig galen.	
Det här vädret gör mig galen.	*This weather* drives me crazy.
Har du köpt alla *dessa saker?*	
Har du köpt alla *de här sakerna?*	Have you bought all *these things?*
Jag vill inte se *den filmen.*	
Jag vill inte se *den där filmen.*	I don't want to see *that picture.*
I *det huset* har jag bott.	
I *det där huset* har jag bott.	I have lived in *that house.*
Skaffa mig *de tidningarna!*	
Skaffa mig *de där tidningarna!*	Get me *those papers.*

7 There is no difference in meaning between the two words corresponding to 'this', but "denna (detta, dessa)" is more usual in written Swedish than in the colloquial language where it is ordinarily replaced by "den här (det här, de här)". However, for many people, especially those from southern Sweden, it is normal to use "denna (detta, dessa)" also in colloquial style.

8 The two pronouns corresponding to 'that' are not always interchangeable. "Den där (det där, de där)" is demonstrative in a more concrete sense: usually it really points to something which is present or at least perceptible or concrete, while "den (det, de)" is often preferred when the noun referred to or qualified is absent or is of a more abstract nature. The distinction is far from clear, however.

Rör inte *den där blomman!*	Don't touch *that flower!* (You are looking at the flower, perhaps pointing to it.)
Rör inte *den blomman!*	Don't touch *that flower!* (You are speaking of a flower you don't see.)
De där knivarna är rostiga.	*Those knives* are rusty. (Looking or pointing at them.)
De knivarna är rostiga.	*Those knives* are rusty. (Just speaking of them.)
Jag ska aldrig glömma *det ögon-blicket.*	I shall never forget *that moment.*
Har du alltid haft *den åsikten?*	Have you always been of *that opinion?*

99 The form "denne" is always used instead of "denna" when it is a "pronoun" (i.e. not followed by a noun) referring to a masculine word. In the written language it is — like "denna", "detta", and "dessa" — often used in the sense of 'the latter'. In that case it usually corresponds to a personal pronoun in English.

Studenten skrev flera brev till den berömde författaren, men *denne* svarade inte.	The student wrote several letters to the famous author but *he* (*the latter*) did not answer.

100 "Den här" and "den där" (and their neuter forms) often correspond to 'this one' and 'that one' in English. Thus the word 'one' should be left out when these expressions are translated into Swedish.

Jag menade inte *den här* utan *den där.*	I didn't mean *this one* but *that one.*

As for 'this' or 'that' followed by 'be' + predicative noun, see above § 72 Note 2.

101 The expressions "så här" and "så där" correspond to 'like this' and 'like that':

Vi kan inte lämna huset *så här.*	We cannot leave the house *like this.*
Skrik inte *så där.*	Don't shout *like that.*

2 In some expressions of time 'this' is rendered by a preposition in Swedish, e.g.: "i år" ('this year'), "i morse" ('this morning'). See further § 265.B.4.

3 **Translation of 'the same'**

A. *'The same'* followed by a noun is rendered by *"samma"* (inflexible). The following noun takes the indefinite form (cp. § 52.3). Thus in this case 'the' in 'the same' is not translated.

Samma kväll såg jag honom utanför biblioteket.	*The same evening* I saw him outside the library.
Vi använder *samma böcker* i år.	We use *the same books* this year.

B. When 'the same' is not followed by a noun it is rendered by "densamma" (neuter: "detsamma", plur.: "desamma"; referring to a masculine noun often "densamme").

Det gör *detsamma.*	It is all *the same.*
Han är alltid *densamme.*	He is always *the same.*

4 **Translation of 'such'**

"Sådan", which is the most common word for 'such', is declined like an adjective in the indefinite form (neuter: *"sådant"*; plural: *"sådana"*). When combined with the indefinite article, "sådan" comes after the article.

Vi säljer inte *sådana böcker* här.	We don't sell *such books* here.
Jag har aldrig sett *ett sådant djur* förr.	I have never seen *such an animal* before.

Note 1. In the spoken language "sådan, sådant, sådana" are often contracted to "sån, sånt, såna".

Note 2. "Sådan" may also correspond to "what" in exclamations (cp. § 116).

En så(da)n stilig karl!	*What a* handsome man!
Så(da)na idéer!	*What* ideas!

Determinative Pronouns and Adjectives

105 *"Den"* (neuter: *"det"*; plural: *"de"*) is also used as a determinative pronoun or adjective, i.e. as a pronominal word referring to a following phrase. This following phrase is usually a relative clause in Swedish (although infinitives and prepositional expressions may also be referred to by a determinative word).

106 *The determinative adjective* "den (det, de)" renders 'the' in English, in the plural sometimes 'those'. The noun preceded by the determinative often takes the indefinite form. When the following relative clause "is necessary" (cannot be left out) the noun following the determinative adjective *must* be in the indefinite form (cp. § 52.2).

Det parti som arbetade för denna reform blev mycket populärt.	*The party that* worked for this reform became very popular.
De elever som kom för sent fick vänta i tamburen.	*The students (those students) who* were late had to wait in the hall.

107 'The' + noun in English (e.g. 'the chair') followed by a relative clause may correspond to either *noun + definite article* (*"stolen"*) or *determinative adjective + noun* (*"den stol"*) in Swedish. The second translation must be used when 'the' + noun are followed by a relative clause (or other phrase referred to) which is "necessary".

Mannen som står där borta är en känd skådespelare. *Den man som* står där borta är en känd skådespelare.	*The man who* is standing over there is a well-known actor.
Jag kommer att vara här *den dag* (*som*) du bestämmer.	I shall be here on *the day* you decide.

)8 *The determinative pronoun* is declined like the corresponding personal pronouns.

	Subj. form	*Obj. form*
Non-neuter	den	den
Neuter	det	det
Plural	de	dem

)9 In cases where Swedish has a determinative pronoun English may have 'that, those', 'the one(s)', 'he, him', 'she, her', 'anyone', or a noun (e.g. 'the man').

Säg till *dem* som ringer, att jag är upptagen.	Tell *those* who phone that I am busy.
Damen där borta är *den*, som A. talade om igår.	The lady over there is *the one* that A. spoke of yesterday.
Den som lever får se.	*He* who lives will see.
Den som begår ett sådant brott förtjänar sitt straff.	*The man* (*Anyone*) who commits such a crime deserves to be punished.

10 Where English uses a determinative pronoun before a noun in the possessive case ('that of ...') Swedish uses a plain possessive.

Månens ljus är blekare än *solens*.	The light of the moon is paler than *that of the sun*.

11 Note that the words "den, det, de" are used in four different ways in Swedish:

1. corresponding to 'the' as additional definite article before adjectives [§ 45];
2. corresponding to 'it' or 'they' as personal pronouns [§§ 71, 72, 73, 74];
3. corresponding to 'that', 'those' as demonstratives [§§ 95, 96, 98];
4. as determinatives.

Interrogative Pronouns and Adjectives

Vem, vad, vilken

112 The principal interrogative pronouns are:

vem (= 'who(m)'; indeclinable)
vad (= 'what'; indeclinable)
vilken (non-neuter), **vilket** (neuter), **vilka** (plural)
(= 'which', 'who' or 'what')

113 "Vad" is not used in the possessive case; the others form their possessive by adding an -s (e.g. "vems").

114 "Vem" is used to translate 'who' when it refers to one person. In cases where 'who' refers to a plural, Swedish uses "vilka".

Vem är den där *flickan?*	*Who* is that *girl?*
Vilka är de där *pojkarna?*	*Who* are those *boys?*

115 "Vad" cannot usually be used as an adjective but only as a pronoun (i.e. it cannot be followed by a noun). The English interrogative adjective 'what' must be translated with "vilken (vilket, vilka)".

Vad ska vi göra?	*What* shall we do?
Vilken bok vill du ha?	*What book* do you want?

116 "Vilken (vilket, vilka)" is used both as a pronoun and as an adjective, both in the singular and the plural. It is also used in exclamations corresponding to 'what a(n)' or 'what'.

Vilka böcker tycker du bäst om?	*Which books* do you like best?
Vilket av husen är ert?	*Which of the houses* is yours?
Vilken stilig karl!	*What a handsome man!*
Vilka idéer!	*What ideas!*

Note. 'What' in exclamations can also be translated by "sådan". For examples, see § 104, note 2.

Vem som, vad som, vilken som

7 When the interrogative pronouns serve as subjects of a dependent clause they must be followed by the relative pronoun "som". (This "som" has no equivalent in English; such words are sometimes called "pleonastic words". Thus "som" in this function is called "the pleonastic som".)

Han frågade mig, *vem som* hade gjort det.
but
Han frågade mig, *vem* jag hade talat med.

He asked me *who* had done it.

He asked me *whom* I had spoken to. ("Vem" is not the subject of the clause.)

Vem har gjort det?

Who has done it? (The clause is independent.)

Jag undrar, *vad som* har hänt.
but
Jag undrar, *vad* han vill.

I wonder *what* has happened.

I wonder *what* he wants.

Vet du, *vilka som* ska komma?
but
Vilka ska komma?

Do you know *who* are coming?

Who are coming?

8 This rule applies to the interrogative adjective "vilken (vilket, vilka)" as well. If it qualifies the subject of a dependent clause, the subject is followed by the pleonastic "som".

Kan ni säga mig, *vilken väg som* är kortast.

Can you tell me *which way* is the shortest.

9 A special interrogative word *"vilkendera"* (neuter: *"vilketdera"*; no plural), is sometimes used corresponding to the English 'which' or 'which one' with a selective meaning (i.e. 'which' out of two or several). It is used both as an adjective and as a pronoun.

Vilkendera vill du ha?
Vilketdera systemet är mest praktiskt?

Which (one) do you want?
Which system is the most practical?

120 There are several Swedish expressions corresponding to the English 'What kind of ...'. The most common are the expressions *"vad för slags"* and *"vad för sorts"*. An interrogative adjective *"hurdan"* (neuter: *"hurdant"*; plural: *"hurdana"*) is usually interchangeable with these expressions.

Vad för slags bläck använder du? ⎫
Vad för sorts bläck använder du? ⎬ *What sort of ink* do you use?
Hurdant bläck använder du? ⎭

121 There is also an interrogative expression *"vad för"* or *"vad för en"* with about the same meaning as "vad för slags". Its non-neuter form is "vad för en" or "vad för", its neuter form "vad för ett" or "vad för", and its plural form "vad för" (sometimes "vad för ena"). Often "vad" and "för" are separated by other words.

Vad för (ett) vin dricker du? ⎫
Vad dricker du *för (ett) vin?* ⎬ *What kind of wine* do you drink?
Vad för slags vin dricker du? ⎬
Vad dricker du *för slags vin?* ⎭

Vad för (sorts) böcker läser hon? ⎫
Vad läser hon *för (sorts) böcker?* ⎬ *What sort of books* does she read?

122 Under the influence of the "vad för"-expressions the phrases *"vad ... för något"* and *"vad ... för nånting"*, corresponding to 'what', are widely used in the colloquial language. "Något" and "nånting", literally meaning 'something', are here pleonastic (i.e. cannot be translated into English). Although these expressions are very common in colloquial style it is never necessary to use them; "vad" alone is enough as a translation of 'what'.

Vad gör du *för något?* ⎫
Vad gör du? ⎬ *What* are you doing?

Vad sjöng hon *för nånting?* ⎫
Vad sjöng hon? ⎬ *What* did she sing?

123 For the similar expression "var ... nånstans", see § 230. B. Note.

Indefinite Pronouns and Adjectives

Some of the Swedish indefinite pronouns and adjectives offer special grammatical problems, others have a use which is similar to that of their English equivalents. Below are discussed only those which are likely to offer difficulties to an English-speaking student.

Ingen (with compound forms)

24 *"Ingen"* (neuter: *"inget"* or *"intet"*; plural: *"inga"*) corresponds to 'no', 'no one', 'nobody', or 'none'. It is used both as an adjective and as a pronoun.

Vi hade *inget vatten.*	We had *no water.*
Han har *inga vänner.*	He has *no friends.*
Ingen lyssnade på mig.	*Nobody* listened to me.
Ingen av de här hattarna passar mig.	*None of* these hats suits me.

25 *"Ingenting"* corresponds to 'nothing'. It is neuter; consequently, an adjective qualifying "ingenting" must take its neuter form.

Han hade *ingenting särskilt* att säga.	He had *nothing particular* to say.
Ingenting är *gott* nog åt honom.	*Nothing* is *good* enough for him.

26 *"Ingendera"* (neuter: *"ingetdera"* or *"intetdera"*; no plural) corresponds to 'neither'.

Ingen(dera) av hennes *föräldrar* kunde komma.	*Neither of her parents* could come.

Translation of 'no', 'no one', etc. in dependent clauses

27 In dependent clauses, 'no', 'no one', 'nobody', 'none', and 'nothing' cannot, without change of word order, be translated by "ingen,

ingenting", but must be rendered by "inte någon", "inte någonting". "Inte" is then placed before the verb (about the place of "inte", see §§ 290, 291).

Eftersom han *inte hade några pengar*, kunde han inte gå på bio.	As he *had no money*, he could not go to the movies.
Jag frågade henne, om det *inte var något* vi kunde göra.	I asked her if there *was nothing* we could do.

This is because a negative word must be placed before the predicative verb in dependent clauses. Thus, with change of word order in the first sentence above, 'no money' may be translated by "inga pengar" which is then placed before the verb:

Eftersom han *inga pengar hade*, kunde han inte gå på bio.	As he *had no money* he could not go to the movies.

This construction is not so common, however.

128 The same splitting of 'no', 'no one', 'nobody', 'none', and 'nothing' into "inte någon", "inte någonting" takes place in independent clauses with compound verb forms. "Inte" is then placed before the second verb form (an infinitive, a supine or participle).

Jag *kan inte se något skäl* att vägra.	I *can see no reason* to refuse.
Jag *har inte träffat någon* som inte tycker om honom.	I *have met no one* who does not like him.

Någon (with compound forms)

129 "*Någon*" (neuter: "*något*"; plural: "*några*") corresponds to 'some', 'somebody', 'someone', 'any', 'anybody', 'anyone'. It is used both as a pronoun and as an adjective.

Någon måste ha varnat honom.	*Somebody* must have warned him.
Några av dem var mycket trötta.	*Some of them* were very tired.
Tala inte om det för *någon*.	Do not tell *anybody* about it.
Finns det *något vatten* i brunnen?	Is there *any water* in the well?

0 *Någonting* (colloquially: "nånting") corresponds to 'something' or 'anything'. It is neuter (cp. § 125).

Hörde du *någonting?* Did you hear *anything?*

Det är *någonting underligt* i den There is *something strange* about
här saken. this matter.

1 "*Någondera*" (neuter: "*någotdera*"; no plural) corresponds to 'either'.

Jag har inte träffat *någon(dera) av* I have not met *either of his sisters.*
hans systrar.

2 As is shown above "någon" with compound forms renders not only 'some', 'somebody', etc. but it may also be the equivalent of 'any', 'anybody', etc. Thus it is used not only in affirmative clauses but also in negative and interrogative ones. As for the translation of 'any' (with compound forms) into Swedish see below § 136.

Note 1. 'Some' used in a partitive sense is often translated by "lite" (literally 'a little'): "Kan jag få *lite vatten*". ('May I have *some water*, please'.)

Note 2. "Några" often corresponds to 'a few': "Jag kommer tillbaka *om några minuter*". ('I shall be back *in a few minutes*'.)

Vem som helst, vad som helst, vilken som helst

3 "*Vem som helst*" (inflexible) corresponds to 'anybody" when 'anybody' means 'anybody you like', 'just anybody', 'everybody'.

Vem som helst kan lösa det här *Anybody* can solve this problem.
problemet.
Han är inte *vem som helst.* He is not *just anybody.*

4 "*Vad som helst*" (inflexible) corresponds to 'anything' when 'anything' means 'anything whatever', 'everything'.

De här djuren äter *vad som helst.* These animals eat *anything.*
Vad vill du ha till middag? — What do you want for dinner? —
Vad som helst. *Anything.*

135 *"Vilken som helst"* (neuter: *"vilket som helst"*; plural: *"vilka som helst"*) corresponds to 'any' or 'anyone', in the sense of 'any(one) you like', 'every-(one)', 'any – – – whatsoever'. It is used both as a pronoun and as an adjective. When "vilken som helst" is used as an adjective "vilken" is placed *before* the noun it qualifies, and "som helst" *after* the noun.

Ni kan få *vilket som helst av de här fotografierna.*	You can have *anyone of these photos.*
Han använder *vilka metoder som helst.*	He uses *any methods whatsoever.*
Vilken skolpojke som helst skulle göra det här bättre än du.	*Any schoolboy* would do this better than you.

Rules for the Translation of "any"

136 The rules for the translation of 'any' (with compound forms) into Swedish could be summarized in the following way:

a) When the basic meaning of the clause is negative or interrogative, or expresses uncertainty or doubt, 'any' (with compound forms) should be translated by "någon" (with compound forms).

Negative:

Han talade inte med någon.	He did not speak to anybody.

Interrogative:

Har du några pengar?	Do you have any money?

Expressing uncertainty:

Om någon kommer, är det bäst att du går.	If anyone comes you had better leave.

Note. 'Any' preceding a comparative form is not translated: "Jag kan inte vänta *längre*". ('I cannot wait *any longer*').

b) When the basic meaning of the clause is affirmative, 'any' (with compound forms) should be translated by "vilken som helst" ,"vem som helst", or "vad som helst". In such cases expressions such as '– – –you like', 'whatsoever', etc. can often be added in English. (For examples see §§ 133–135 above.)

Note. "Vad som helst" may also be used in negative clauses in the sense of 'everything', 'just anything':

Jag äter *inte vad som helst*. I do *not* eat *just anything*.

37 The "... *som helst*"-expressions followed by "*som*" are called indefinite relative pronouns. "Vem som helst som" corresponds to 'whoever', "vad som helst som" to 'whatever', etc.

Vem som helst som har besökt Stock- *Whoever* has visited Stockholm
holm vet, att ... knows that ...

Man

38 "*Man*" (possessive: "*ens*"; object form: "*en*") corresponds to German 'man' and French 'on'; it has no real equivalent in English, although 'one' could be used as a basic translation. It is often used in cases where English would have 'you', 'they', 'people', or a passive construction (i.e. passive voice of the predicate verb and no equivalent of "man").

Man bör inte misströsta. *One* ought not to despair.
Man får inte röka här. *You* must not smoke here.
Man dricker mycket kaffe i Sve- *We* drink a great deal of coffee in
rige. Sweden.
Man säger, att de ska gifta sig. *They* (*People*) *say* that they are
  going to marry.
Man säger, att hon är mycket för- *She is said* to be very wealthy.
mögen.
Man höjde lönerna. The wages *were raised*.

Annan

39 "*Annan*" corresponds to 'other' and 'else'. It is declined like an adjective; its neuter form is "*annat*" and its plural and definite form "*andra*":

annan, annat other
andra other, others
en annan, ett annat another (one)

den andra, det andra, de andra	the other (one, ones)
de andra	the others

När Ulf hade gått, kom *en annan pojke* fram till mig.	When Ulf had left *another boy* came up to me.
Det andra rummet är mycket bättre.	*The other room* is much better.
Den där stolen är sönder; ta *den andra* i stället.	That chair is broken; take *the other one* instead.
Var är *de andra?*	Where are *the others?*
Jag vill hellre ha *någonting annat.*	I prefer to have *something else.*

Note 1. The expression 'one . . . the other' is in Swedish "den ena . . . den andra": "*Den ena efter den andra* började gäspa" ('*One after the other* began to yawn').

Note 2. The expressions 'the other day', 'the other night' are rendered in Swedish by "häromdagen", "häromkvällen": "Jag träffade Kalle *häromdagen*" ('I met Charlie *the other day*').

Translation of 'another'

140 In translating 'another' into Swedish it is important to make clear whether it means 'different, of another kind' or 'additional'. 'Another' in the sense of 'a different' is "*en annan*" or "*ett annat*", while 'another' in the sense of 'an additional' is translated by "*en . . . till*" or "*ett . . . till*".

Jag vill ha *en annan bil.*	I want *another* (i.e. a different) *car.*
Jag vill ha *en bil till.*	I want *another car* (i.e. in addition to the one I have).
Läs texten *en gång till.*	Read the text *once more* ("*another time*").
Vi har sålt vår gamla båt och köpt *en annan* i stället.	We have sold our old boat and bought *another one* instead.

All, allting

1 "*All*" (neuter: "*allt*"; plural: "*alla*") corresponds to 'all'.

Han fick *all den hjälp* han behövde.	He got *all the help* he needed.
Allt hopp är ute.	*All hope* is gone.
De förlorade *alla sina pengar*.	They lost *all their money*.
Är *vi alla* här?	Are *we all* here?

"*Alla*" often renders 'every, everybody'. See §§ 147, 148.

2 "*Allting*" corresponds to 'everything'. It is neuter (cp. § 125) and usually interchangeable with "allt".

Allt(ing) verkar vara mycket dyrt här.	*Everything* seems to be very expensive here.
Har du berättat *allt(ing)* för henne?	Have you told her *everything?*

3 English 'all' or 'all the' in the sense of 'the whole' is translated by "*hela*" (followed by noun in the definite form; cp. § 48. Note).

Hela dagen.	*All day.*
Hela tiden.	*All the time.*

Varje, var, varenda, var och en

4 "*Varje*" (inflexible) corresponds to 'every' and 'each'. It is used mainly as an adjective. "Varje" is sometimes replaced by a shorter form, "*var*" (neuter: "*vart*"), with the same meaning. This latter word must be used before an ordinal number and in the sense of 'each' when no noun follows.

Varje morgon tar jag en promenad.	*Every morning* I take a walk.
Valet äger rum *vart fjärde år.*	The election takes place *every four years* (literally: every fourth year).
Vi fick *två biljetter var.*	We got *two tickets each.*

Note. 'Every other', 'every second' is *"varannan"* (neuter: *"vartannat"*).

Han kommer hit *vartannat år*.　　He comes here *every second year*.

145 *"Varenda"* (neuter: *"vartenda"*) is another equivalent of 'every', 'each'. It is used as an adjective. Usually, it is more emphatic than "varje". The corresponding pronoun is *"varenda en"* (= 'everyone').

Jag hittade fel på *varenda rad*.

I found errors on *each and every line*.

När jag var ung, kunde jag många visor, men nu har jag glömt *varenda en*.

When I was young I knew many songs, but now I have forgotten *every one*.

146 *"Var och en"* (neuter: *"vart och ett"*) corresponds to 'everybody', 'everyone', 'each'. It is used as a pronoun.

Polisen förhörde *var och en* mycket ingående.

The police interrogated *everybody* very closely.

However, as a translation of 'everybody', 'everyone', "alla" is more common than "var och en".

Är *alla* här?　　*Is everyone* here?

Alla tycker om henne.　　*Everybody* likes her.

147 "Alla" is also used frequently to translate 'every'.

På *alla sätt*.　　In *every way*.

Åt *alla håll*.　　In *every direction*.

148 **Reciprocal Pronoun**

Vi har sett *varandra* förut.　　We have seen *each other* before.

Flickorna lånar *varandras* kläder.　　The girls borrow *one another's* clothes.

English 'each other', 'one another' is rendered in Swedish by *"varandra"* (possessive form: *"varandras"*). Note that reciprocal action can also sometimes be expressed with the s-form of the verb. Cp § 191.

VERBS

Introduction

Remarks on English Verb Forms

149 In English it is, as a rule, sufficient to give three principal parts of the verb, namely the infinitive, the past tense and the past participle, e.g.:

Infinitive	*Past Tense*	*Past Participle*
go	went	gone

With these three forms, most tenses can be formed:

Present: I go
Past: I went
Present Perfect: I have gone
Past Perfect: I had gone
Future: I shall go
Conditional: I should go

Only in exceptional cases is it necessary in English to give also the present tense form of the verb:

Infinitive	*Present Tense*	*Past Tense*	*Past Participle*
be	am, are, is	was, were	been

Note 1. As a rule, English verbs have the same form for the *infinitive* and the *present tense*, except in the third person: he goes.

Note 2. For the majority of English verbs the form of the *past tense* is identical with that of the *past participle*, e.g.:

Infinitive	*Past Tense*	*Past Participle*
have	had	had
work	worked	worked

Remarks on Swedish Verb Forms

50 In modern Swedish the **infinitive** and the **present tense** have separate forms.

The infinitive of the majority of Swedish verbs ends in *-a*:
att ha ('to have'), *att vara* ('to be'), *att baka* ('to bake').

The present tense of almost all verbs (for exceptions, see §§ 159–162, 171) ends in *-r*: *jag har* ('I have'), *jag är* ('I am'), *jag bakar* ('I bake').

151 The **past tense** in Swedish has a separate form from the **past participle.**

The past tense of the majority of verbs ends in *-de* or *-te*:
jag hade ('I had'), *jag bakade* ('I baked'), *jag köpte* ('I bought').

152 There are *two verb forms* in Swedish corresponding to the English past participle:

1. **The Supine.** This is used with forms of the auxiliary verb "ha" ('have') to form the present perfect and past perfect tenses:

Jag *har bakat* en kaka. I *have baked* a cake.
Jag *hade bakat* en kaka. I *had baked* a cake.

2. **The Past Participle.** This is used with forms of the auxiliary verbs "bliva, vara" ('become, be') to form the passive voice, and also as an adjective:

Kakan *är bakad* idag. The cake *is baked* today.
En *hembakad* kaka. A *home-baked* cake.

153 The past participle is declined according to gender and number:

Kakan är *bakad* idag. (Non-neuter) The cake is baked today.

Brödet är *bakat* idag. (Neuter) The bread is baked today.

Kakorna } är *bakade* idag. (Plural) The cakes } are baked today.
Bröden } The pastries }

For a table of the endings of the past participle in the four conjugations, see § 180.

54 For a table of the endings of the principal parts of the verbs in the four conjugations, see § 165.

55 In modern Swedish there is *one form* for all persons in the present and past tenses of verbs:

jag		I	**am**	jag		I	**was**
du		you	**are**	du		you	**were**
han		he		han		he	
hon		she		hon		she	
den	**är**	it	**is**	den	**var**	it	**was**
det		it		det		it	
vi		we		vi		we	
ni		you	**are**	ni		you	**were**
de		they		de		they	

For remarks on the plural forms of verbs see § 166.

Auxiliary Verbs

56 **Translation of English 'Do' + Principal Verb**

There is no auxiliary verb in Swedish corresponding to English 'do'. 'Do' + a principal verb in English is translated into Swedish by the simple principal verb:

Bor du här?	*Do* you *live* here?
Var *såg* du honom?	Where *did* you *see* him?
Jag *förstår inte* riktigt.	I *do not* quite *understand*.
Jag *hittade inte* gatan.	I *did not find* the street.
Kom någon gång!	*Do come* some time!

57 **Remarks on the Following Verb Paradigms**

In the following verb paradigms *the future tense* is formed by "ska(ll)" + the infinitive of the verb. Note that the future tense is often rendered by "kommer att" + infinitive. Cp. § 195. n. 2.

158 **att ha** to have

Principal Parts:

Infinitive	Present Tense	Past Tense	Supine	Past Participle
ha	**har**	**hade**	**haft**	(-havd)

PRESENT TENSE	PAST TENSE	PRESENT PERFECT TENSE	PAST PERFECT TENSE
I have *etc.*	I had *etc.*	I have had *etc.*	I had had *etc.*
jag du han hon den } **har** det vi ni de	jag du han hon den } **hade** det vi ni de	jag du han hon den } **har haft** det vi ni de	jag du han hon den } **hade haft** det vi ni de

FUTURE TENSE	CONDITIONAL TENSE
I shall have *etc.*	I should have *etc.*
jag du han hon den } **ska(ll) ha** det vi ni de	jag du han hon den } **skulle ha** det vi ni de

9 **att vara** to be

Principal Parts:

Infinitive	Present Tense	Past Tense	Supine	Past Participle
vara	**är**	**var**	**varit**	—

PRESENT TENSE	PAST TENSE	PRESENT PERFECT TENSE	PAST PERFECT TENSE
I am *etc.*	I was *etc.*	I have been *etc.*	I had been *etc.*
jag du han hon den } **är** det vi ni de	jag du han hon den } **var** det vi ni de	jag du han hon den } **har varit** det vi ni de	jag du han hon den } **hade varit** det vi ni de

FUTURE TENSE I shall be *etc.*	CONDITIONAL TENSE I should be *etc.*
jag du han hon den } **ska(ll) vara** det vi ni de	jag du han hon den } **skulle vara** det vi ni de

106 ska(ll) shall, will

Principal Parts:

Infinitive	Present Tense	Past Tense	Supine	Past Participle
skola	**ska(ll)**	**skulle**	—	—

Present Tense	Past Tense
I *shall, will etc.*	I *should, would etc.*

jag			jag	
du			du	
han			han	
hon			hon	
den	**ska(ll)**		den	**skulle**
det			det	
vi			vi	
ni			ni	
de			de	

Note. The present tense form of the verb is written "skall" or "ska". It is always pronounced "ska".

161 kan *can*

Principal Parts:

Infinitive	Present Tense	Past Tense	Supine	Past Participle
kunna	**kan**	**kunde**	**kunnat**	—

Present Tense	Past Tense
jag **kan** *I can*	jag **kunde** *I could*
du **kan** *you can*	du **kunde** *you could*
etc.	*etc.*

162 måste *must*

Principal Parts:

—	**måste**	**måste**	—	—

Present Tense	Past Tense	Future Tense
jag **måste** *I must*	jag **måste** *I had to*	jag **måste** *I shall have to*
etc.	*etc.*	*etc.*

63 **vill** *want to [do something]*

Principal parts:

Infinitive	Present Tense	Past Tense	Supine	Past Participle
vilja	**vill**	**ville**	**velat**	—

Present Tense		Past Tense	
jag **vill**	*I want to*	jag **ville**	*I wanted to*
du **vill**	*you want to*	du **ville**	*you wanted to*
etc.	*etc.*	*etc.*	*etc.*

64 For the auxiliaries "*att bli*" ('to be, become'), "*bör*" ('ought to'), "*får*" ('may'), "*att låta*" ('to let') see § 171.

Main Verbs

Conjugations

65 There are four main groups of Swedish verbs, characterized by four patterns of endings. These are *the four conjugations.*

In the first, second, and third conjugations the different tenses are formed by the addition of endings to the infinitive stem of the verb (the infinitive minus -*a*, e.g. **bak**|a ('bake'). In the third conjugation the endings are added to the full infinitive form.

In the fourth conjugation the present tense ending is added to the stem of the infinitive. No ending is added in the past tense. This is formed instead by change of the stem vowel. The supine and past participle endings of some groups of verbs within this conjugation are added to a stem different from that of the infinitive, containing another vowel than the infinitive. See further § 171.

The following is a table of the endings of the principal parts of the verbs in the four conjugations:

	INFINITIVE	PRESENT TENSE	PAST TENSE	SUPINE	PAST PARTICIPLE /non-neuter form/
1st conj.	-a	-ar	-ade	-at	-ad
2nd conj.	1) -a	-er	-de	-t	-d
	2) -a	-er	-te	-t	-t
3rd conj.	-	-r	-dde	-tt	-dd
4th conj.	-a	-er	-	-it	-en

166 Remarks on Plural Forms of Verbs

There are special plural forms of verbs in the present and past tenses. They are falling out of use, however, and are now found only in formal style. It is never necessary to use the plural forms of verbs.

The present tense plural form is the same as the infinitive of the verb, e.g.: *"vi ha, ni ha, de ha"* ('we have, you have, they have'), *"vi sjunga, ni sjunga, de sjunga"* ('we sing, you sing, they sing'). Past tense plural verb forms are found only among verbs of the fourth conjugation and some irregular verbs (not belonging to any of the four main conjugations). These forms are always disyllabic and end in -o. For some verbs these forms contain the same stem vowel as the past tense singular form, for other verbs the stem vowel of the supine and past participle forms. A few irregular verbs have past tense plural forms made from stems other than either of these forms. Examples of these different past tense plural forms are given in the table below.

INFINITIVE	PRESENT TENSE	PAST TENSE *Sing.*	PAST TENSE *Plur.*	SUPINE	PAST PARTICIPLE
sjunga ('sing')	sjunger	sjöng	**sjöngo**	sjungit	sjungen
dricka ('drink')	dricker	drack	**drucko**	druckit	drucken
få ('get, receive, may')	får	fick	**fingo**	fått	—
vara ('be')	är[1]	var	**voro**	varit	—

[1] The present tense plural form of "vara" is "äro": *"Vi äro, ni äro, de äro"* ('We are, you are, they are').

First Conjugation

167 **att baka** to bake

Principal Parts:

Infinitive	Present Tense	Past Tense	Supine	Past Participle
baka	**bakar**	**bakade**	**bakat**	**bakad**

PRESENT TENSE	PAST TENSE	PRESENT PERFECT TENSE	PAST PERFECT TENSE
I bake *etc.*	I baked *etc.*	I have baked *etc.*	I had baked *etc.*
jag du han hon den } **bakar** det vi ni de	jag du han hon den } **bakade** det vi ni de	jag du han hon den } **har bakat** det vi ni de	jag du han hon den } **hade bakat** det vi ni de

FUTURE TENSE I shall bake *etc.*	CONDITIONAL TENSE I should bake *etc.*
jag du han hon den } **ska(ll) baka** det vi ni de	jag du han hon den } **skulle baka** det vi ni de

Note. Nearly half of the most common Swedish verbs belong to this conjugation. New verbs that are introduced into Swedish take the endings of the first conjugation, e.g. *missa* ('fail, miss [the train]'), *lifta* ('hitch-hike').

Second Conjugation (Group 1)

68 **att ställa** to put

Principal Parts:

Infinitive	Present Tense	Past Tense	Supine	Past Participle
ställa	**ställer**	**ställde**	**ställt**	**ställd**

PRESENT TENSE	PAST TENSE	PRESENT PERFECT TENSE	PAST PERFECT TENSE
I put *etc.*	I put *etc.*	I have put *etc.*	I had put *etc.*
jag du han hon den } **ställer** det vi ni de	jag du han hon den } **ställde** det vi ni de	jag du han hon den } **har ställt** det vi ni de	jag du han hon den } **hade ställt** det vi ni de

FUTURE TENSE I shall put *etc.*	CONDITIONAL TENSE I should put *etc.*
jag du han hon den } **ska(ll) ställa** det vi ni de	jag du han hon den } **skulle ställa** det vi ni de

Second Conjugation (Group 2)

att köpa to buy

Principal Parts:

Infinitive	Present Tense	Past Tense	Supine	Past Participle
köpa	**köper**	**köpte**	**köpt**	**köpt**

PRESENT TENSE	PAST TENSE	PRESENT PERFECT TENSE	PAST PERFECT TENSE
I buy *etc.*	I bought *etc.*	I have bought *etc.*	I had bought *etc.*
jag du han hon den } **köper** det vi ni de	jag du han hon den } **köpte** det vi ni de	jag du han hon den } **har köpt** det vi ni de	jag du han hon den } **hade köpt** det vi ni de

FUTURE TENSE	CONDITIONAL TENSE
I shall buy *etc.*	I should buy *etc.*
jag du han hon den } **ska(ll) köpa** det vi ni de	jag du han hon den } **skulle köpa** det vi ni de

Remarks on the Second Conjugation

In the second conjugation there are two groups of verbs.

1. The verbs of the first group have a past tense form ending in *-de* and a past participle ending in *-d*. To this group belong verbs whose stem ends in a voiced consonant.

2. The verbs of the second group have a past tense form ending in *-te* and a past participle ending in *-t*. To this group belong verbs whose stem ends in a voiceless consonant (k, p, s, t).

Note 1. Verbs whose stem ends in *-r* drop the present tense ending *-er*, e.g.:

Infinitive	Present Tense	Past Tense	Supine	Past Participle
höra ('hear')	**hör**	hörde	hört	hörd
köra ('drive')	**kör**	körde	kört	körd
lära ('learn')	**lär**	lärde	lärt	lärd

Note 2. In verbs whose stem ends in a *vowel + d* 'd' is changed into 't' before the supine ending:

föda ('bear')	föder	födde	**fött**	född
råda ('advise')	råder	rådde	**rått**	rådd

Note 3. Verbs whose infinitives end in *-nda* drop the 'd' before the past tense and past participle endings and also before the supine 't'.

vända ('turn')	vänder	**vände**	**vänt**	**vänd**

Note 4. Concerning the dropping of one 'm' or 'n' in the past tense, supine and past participle forms of verbs like "glömma" ('forget'), "känna" ('know, feel'), see § 15.

Third Conjugation

69 att tro to believe

Principal Parts:

Infinitive	Present Tense	Past Tense	Supine	Past Participle
tro	**tror**	**trodde**	**trott**	**trodd**

PRESENT TENSE	PAST TENSE	PRESENT PERFECT TENSE	PAST PERFECT TENSE
I believe *etc.*	I believed *etc.*	I have believed *etc.*	I had believed *etc.*
jag du han hon den } **tror** det vi ni de	jag du han hon den } **trodde** det vi ni de	jag du han hon den } **har trott** det vi ni de	jag du han hon den } **hade trott** det vi ni de

FUTURE TENSE I shall believe *etc.*	CONDITIONAL TENSE I should believe *etc.*
jag du han hon den } **ska(ll) tro** det vi ni de	jag du han hon den } **skulle tro** det vi ni de

Fourth Conjugation

170 The verbs of the fourth conjugation form their past tense not by an ending but by change of their stem vowel. As in English 'irregular' verbs there are several different types of vowel changes, e.g.:

Infinitive	Present Tense	Past Tense	Supine	Past Participle
dricka (*drink*)	dricker	drack	druckit	drucken
rida (*ride*)	rider	red	ridit	riden

Note. Verbs in this group whose stems end in -r drop the present tense ending -er, e.g. **bära**, han **bär** ('carry, he carries').

171 The following is an *alphabetical list of the verbs of the fourth conjugation including also some common irregular verbs* (not belonging to any of the four main conjugations).

INFINITIVE	PRESENT TENSE	PAST TENSE	SUPINE	PAST PARTICIPLE
be(dja) *ask, pray*	ber	bad	bett	-bedd
binda *bind, tie*	binder	band	bundit	bunden
bita *bite*	biter	bet	bitit	biten
bjuda *offer, invite*	bjuder	bjöd	bjudit	bjuden
bli(va) *become*	bli(ve)r	blev	blivit	bliven
brinna *burn*	brinner	brann	brunnit	brunnen
brista *burst*	brister	brast	brustit	brusten
bryta *break*	bryter	bröt	brutit	bruten

INFINITIVE	PRESENT TENSE	PAST TENSE	SUPINE	PAST PARTICIPLE
bära	bär	bar	burit	buren
carry, wear, bear				
böra	bör	borde	bort	—
ought to				
dra(ga)	dra(ge)r	drog	dragit	dragen
draw, pull				
dricka	dricker	drack	druckit	drucken
drink				
driva	driver	drev	drivit	driven
*drive**				
duga	duger	dugde, dög	dugt	—
do, serve, be fit				
dö	dör	dog	dött	—
die				
dölja	döljer	dolde	dolt	dold
conceal				
falla	faller	föll	fallit	fallen
fall				
fara	far	for	farit	faren
go, travel				
finna	finner	fann	funnit	funnen
find				
finnas	finns	fanns	funnits	—
be, exist				
flyga	flyger	flög	flugit	-flugen
fly				
flyta	flyter	flöt	flutit	-fluten
float				
frysa	fryser	frös	frusit	frusen
freeze				
få	får	fick	fått	—
get (receive), may				

* 'Drive a car' is rendered in Swedish by "köra bil".

INFINITIVE	PRESENT TENSE	PAST TENSE	SUPINE	PAST PARTICIPLE
försvinna *disappear*	försvinner	försvann	försvunnit	försvunnen
gala *crow*	gal	gol	galit	—
ge, giva *give*	ger, giver	gav	gett, givit	given
gjuta *cast*	gjuter	göt	gjutit	gjuten
glida *glide*	glider	gled	glidit	—
glädja *make happy, please*	gläder	gladde	glatt	—
gnida *rub*	gnider	gned	gnidit	gniden
gripa *seize*	griper	grep	gripit	gripen
gråta *cry, weep*	gråter	grät	gråtit	(be)gråten
gå *go, walk*	går	gick	gått	gången
göra *do, make*	gör	gjorde	gjort	gjord
ha(va) *have*	har	hade	haft	-havd
heta *be called*	heter	hette	hetat	—
hinna *have time, attain*	hinner	hann	hunnit	hunnen
hugga *cut, hew*	hugger	högg	huggit	huggen
hålla *hold*	håller	höll	hållit	hållen

Infinitive	Present Tense	Past Tense	Supine	Past Participle
kliva *stride, step, climb*	kliver	klev	klivit	-kliven
klyva *cleave*	klyver	klöv	kluvit	kluven
knyta *tie*	knyter	knöt	knutit	knuten
komma *come*	kommer	kom	kommit	kommen
krypa *creep*	kryper	kröp	krupit	krupen
kunna *be able, may, know*	kan	kunde	kunnat	—
le *smile*	ler	log	lett	—
leva *live*	lever	levde	lev|a|t	-lev(a)d
lida *suffer*	lider	led	lidit	liden
ligga *lie (lay, lain)*	ligger	låg	legat	-legad
ljuda *sound*	ljuder	ljöd	ljudit	—
ljuga *lie (lied, lied)*	ljuger	ljög	ljugit	-ljugen
lyda *run, read, be worded, obey*	lyder	löd, lydde	lytt	-lydd
låta *let, permit, sound*	låter	lät	låtit	-låten
lägga *lay, put*	lägger	lade	lagt	lagd
— *must*	måste	måste	måst	—

Infinitive	Present Tense	Past Tense	Supine	Past Participle
niga *curtsy*	niger	neg	nigit	—
njuta *enjoy*	njuter	njöt	njutit	njuten
nysa *sneeze*	nyser	nös	nyst	—
pipa *pipe*	piper	pep	pipit	—
rida *ride (on horseback)*	rider	red	ridit	riden
rinna *run, flow*	rinner	rann	runnit	runnen
riva *tear*	river	rev	rivit	riven
ryta *roar*	ryter	röt	rutit	—
se *see*	ser	såg	sett	sedd
sitta *sit*	sitter	satt	suttit	-sutten
sjuda *seethe*	sjuder	sjöd	sjudit	sjuden
sjunga *sing*	sjunger	sjöng	sjungit	sjungen
sjunka *sink*	sjunker	sjönk	sjunkit	sjunken
skina *shine*	skiner	sken	skinit	—
skjuta *shoot, push*	skjuter	sköt	skjutit	skjuten
skola *shall*	ska(ll)	skulle	(skolat)	—

INFINITIVE	PRESENT TENSE	PAST TENSE	SUPINE	PAST PARTICIPLE
skrida *glide, proceed*	skrider	skred	skridit	-skriden
skrika *scream, shout*	skriker	skrek	skrikit	-skriken
skriva *write*	skriver	skrev	skrivit	skriven
skryta *boast*	skryter	skröt	skrutit	-skruten
skära *cut*	skär	skar	skurit	skuren
slippa *be spared from*	slipper	slapp	sluppit	-sluppen
slita *tear*	sliter	slet	slitit	sliten
sluta* *close, conclude*	sluter	slöt	slutit	sluten
slå *beat, strike*	slår	slog	slagit	slagen
slåss *fight*	slåss	slogs	slagits	—
smyga *sneak, slip*	smyger	smög	smugit	-smugen
snyta *blow the nose*	snyter	snöt	snutit	snuten
sova *sleep*	sover	sov	sovit	—
spinna *spin*	spinner	spann	spunnit	spunnen

---

* *sluta* can also be a verb of the first conjugation. It then has the meaning 'end, finish, bring to an end, stop', e.g.: Har skolan *slutat* ännu? (Has school finished yet?)

INFINITIVE	PRESENT TENSE	PAST TENSE	SUPINE	PAST PARTICIPLE
spricka *burst, crack*	spricker	sprack	spruckit	sprucken
sprida *spread*	sprider	spred, spridde	spritt	spridd
springa *run*	springer	sprang	sprungit	sprungen
sticka *stick, put*	sticker	stack	stuckit	stucken
stiga *rise, step*	stiger	steg	stigit	-stigen
stjäla *steal*	stjäl	stal	stulit	stulen
strida *fight*	strider	stred	stridit	-stridd
stryka *stroke, iron*	stryker	strök	strukit	struken
stå *stand*	står	stod	stått	-stådd
stödja *support*	stöder	stödde	stött	stödd
supa *drink (liquor)*	super	söp	supit	-supen
svida *smart, ache*	svider	sved	svidit	—
svika *fail*	sviker	svek	svikit	sviken
svälta *starve*	svälter	svalt	svultit	svulten
svär(j)a *swear*	svär	svor	svurit	svuren
säga *say*	säger	sade	sagt	sagd

INFINITIVE	PRESENT TENSE	PAST TENSE	SUPINE	PAST PARTICIPLE
sälja *sell*	säljer	sålde	sålt	såld
sätta *set, put*	sätter	satte	satt	satt
ta(ga) *take*	ta(ge)r	tog	tagit	tagen
tiga *be silent*	tiger	teg	tigit, tegat	-tegen
tjuta *howl*	tjuter	tjöt	tjutit	—
(töras) *dare*	törs	tordes	torts	—
vara *be*	är	var	varit	—
veta *know*	vet	visste	vetat	—
vika *fold*	viker	vek	vikit	viken, vikt
vilja *be willing, want to*	vill	ville	velat	—
vina *whiz*	viner	ven	vinit	—
vinna *win*	vinner	vann	vunnit	vunnen
vrida *twist, twin, turn*	vrider	vred	vridit	vriden
välja *choose, elect*	väljer	valde	valt	vald
vänja *accustom*	vänjer	vande	vant	vand
äta *eat*	äter	åt	ätit	äten

172 There are a great number of compound verbs in Swedish. Below are listed a few whose stems are verbs given in § 171 and which have the same conjugation as these. The stem verb is in bold type.

anse *consider;* ansluta *join;* anta|ga *suppose, accept;* avbryta *interrupt;* avgöra *decide;* bedra|ga *deceive;* bese *inspect;* beskriva *describe;* bestå *consist;* erbjuda *offer;* erhålla *receive;* ersätta *replace;* fortsätta *continue;* förbjuda *forbid;* föredra|ga *prefer;* förekomma *occur;* föreslå *suggest, propose;* förlåta *forgive;* förstå *understand;* inbjuda *invite;* innebära *mean, imply;* motta|ga *receive;* pågå *go on, continue;* tillåta *allow;* undvika *avoid;* uppfinna *invent;* uppstå *arise;* översätta *translate;*

For remarks on compound verbs, see §§ 223–226.

Mood

The Imperative

173 In English the imperative is identical in form with the infinitive:

Infinitive: You must *come* at once.
Imperative: Come here at once!

174 In Swedish the infinitive and the imperative are identical in form for verbs of the *first and the third conjugations* and for irregular verbs whose infinitive does not end in *-a*:

FIRST CONJUGATION

Vänta!	*Wait!*
Tala långsammare!	*Speak* more slowly!

THIRD CONJUGATION

Tro mig!	*Believe* me!

IRREGULAR

Gå till vänster!	*Walk* to the left!
Stå till höger i rulltrappan!	*Stand* to the right on the escalator!

75 For verbs of the *second and fourth conjugations* the imperative is identical with the stem of the verb (infinitive minus *-a*):

SECOND CONJUGATION

Kör sakta!	*Drive* slowly!
Köp vårt goda bröd!	*Buy* our good bread!

FOURTH CONJUGATION

Skjut!	*Push!*
Sov gott!	*Sleep* well!

The Use of the Imperative

76 The imperative is used as in English.

77 In requests it is often more polite to use some paraphrase of the imperative, e.g.:

Var snäll och stäng fönstret!
Stäng fönstret, *(så) är du snäll!* } *Shut* the window, *please.*
Kan ni stänga fönstret!   Can you please *shut* the window.

The Subjunctive

78 There are special subjunctive forms of verbs but they are rarely used. It is never necessary to use the subjunctive.

In the following expressions the verb is in the present tense of the subjunctive. It is formed by adding *-e* to the stem of the verb.

Leve drottningen!	Long *live* the Queen.
Gud *välsigne* dig!	God *bless* you.

In the sentences below the verb is in the past tense form of the subjunctive. It is formed by exchanging the *o*-ending of the past tense plural form (cp. § 166) for an *-e*.

Om jag *finge*, skulle jag absolut göra det.	If I *were allowed to*, I should definitely do it.
Det *vore* roligt att fara till Köpenhamn.	It *would be* nice to go to Copenhagen.

The Participles

The Past Participle

179 The past participle is used after forms of "bli" and "vara" to form the passive voice, and also as an adjective. It is declined according to gender and number.

180 The following is a table of the endings of the past participle in the four conjugations:

	NON-NEUTER (BASIC FORM)	NEUTER	PLURAL AND DEF. FORM
1st conj.	bak|ad	bak|at	bak|ade
2nd conj.	1 ställ|d 2 köp|t	ställ|t köp|t	ställ|da köp|ta
3rd conj.	tro|dd	tro|tt	tro|dda
4th conj.	bjud|en	bjud|et	bjud|na

Note. In the fourth conjugation the past participle ending is added to the stem of the supine: bunden *bound*, frusen *frozen*.

Examples of the use of the past participle:

Allt vårt bröd *är hembakat.*	All our bread *is home-baked.*
Det hembakade brödet är bäst.	The home-baked bread is best.
Jag *är anställd* i Riksbanken.	I *am employed* in the National Bank.
Han *blir* aldrig *trodd.*	He *is* never *believed.*
Huset *är obebott.*	The house *is uninhabited.*
Jag *är bortbjuden* på middag idag.	I *am invited* out for dinner to-day.
Vi har *blivit bjudna* på bröllop nästa månad.	We have *been invited* to a wedding next month.

The Present Participle

31 The present participle in Swedish is mainly used as an *adjective*. It is indeclinable.

32 The following are the endings of the present participle in the four conjugations:

1st conj. bak|ande
2nd conj. ställ|ande, köp|ande
3rd conj. bo|ende
4th conj. bjud|ande

In the *first*, *second* and *fourth* conjugations the present participle is formed by the addition of the ending *-ande* to the stem of the verb. In the *third* conjugation and for irregular verbs whose infinitive does not end in -a, the present participle is formed by the addition of the ending *-ende* to the stem of the verb.

Examples of the use of the present participle:

Det är en *fängslande* bok.	It is a *fascinating* book.
Han höll ett *lysande* tal.	He made a *brilliant* speech.
Hon har en *inneboende* styrka.	She has an *inherent* strength.
Filmen var *underhållande*.	The film was *entertaining*.

Note 1. The present participle is sometimes used as an adverb. For an example of this, see § 231.

Note 2. The present participle, as a rule, cannot be used as a verb. Note, however, § 215.

Note 3. There is no equivalent in Swedish to the English continuous tense. For the translation of the continuous tense, see § 221.

Note 4. The present participle is sometimes changed into a noun, taking noun endings.

Vid *försvinnandet* var han klädd i brun överrock.	At *his disappearance* he was dressed in a brown overcoat.

Passive Voice

183 In English the passive voice is formed by the verb 'be' + the past participle of the principal verb:

Active Voice
A rich man *bóught* the house.

Passive Voice
The house *was bought* by a rich man.

184 In Swedish there are two main ways of forming the passive voice. It can be formed by the verbs "bliva" or "vara" + the past participle *or* by the addition of *-s* to the active form of the verb:

En rik man köpte huset.

Huset $\left\{\begin{array}{l}\textbf{blev köpt}\\\textbf{köptes}\end{array}\right.$ av en rik man.

S-Passive

185 The following table shows the formation of the s-passive in the different conjugations:

	PRESENT TENSE	PAST TENSE	SUPINE
1st conj.	den **bakas** *it is baked*	den **bakades** *it was baked*	den har **bakats** *it has been baked*
2nd conj.	den **ställ(e)s** *it is put* den **köp(e)s** *it is bought*	den **ställdes** *it was put* den **köptes** *is was bought*	den har **ställts** *it has been put* den har **köpts** *it has been bought*
3rd conj.	han **tros** *he is believed*	han **troddes** *he was believed*	han har **trotts** *he has been believed*
4th conj.	den **skriv(e)s** *it is written*	den **skrevs** *it was written*	den har **skrivits** *it has been written*

The passive infinitive is formed by adding *-s* to the active infinitive form of the verb. Thus the future tense is: "den ska (kommer att) **bakas**" ('It will *be baked*') etc.

Compound Passive

86 1. The compound passive is usually formed with forms of "bliva" + the past participle, e.g.:

Hon *blev skadad* i en olycka.   She *was injured* in an accident.

2. The compound passive is sometimes formed with forms of "vara" + the past participle, e.g.:

Hon *var omtyckt* av alla.   She *was well liked* by everybody.

The Use of the S-Passive and the Compound Passive

87 The *s-passive* can usually be used interchangeably with the compound passive. The s-passive, however, is not quite so common in the spoken language.

88 The passive constructions with *"bli"* + *past participle* and *"vara"* + *past participle cannot* be used interchangeably.

1. *"bli"* + *past participle* is the usual compound passive construction. It denotes an action or occurrence which the subject undergoes, e.g.:

Bilen *blev stulen*, medan jag var borta.   The car *was stolen* while I was away.

2. *"vara"* + *past participle* is used as the passive construction for verbs which do not denote action or occurrence, e.g.:

Hon *var omtyckt* av alla.   She *was well liked* by everybody.

89 However, the following English sentence can be translated into Swedish in two ways with different meanings:

The car *was stolen*.   Bilen *blev stulen*.
   Bilen *var stulen*.

This is because the English sentence has two meanings. These can perhaps be illustrated by enlarging the sentence in two ways:

The car *was stolen* while I was away.

Bilen *blev stulen*, medan jag var borta.

The car *was stolen* when I came back.

Bilen *var stulen*, när jag kom tillbaka.

In the first example the verb is in the passive voice to describe the *occurrence* of the stealing of the car. The verb in English can be changed into active voice in the same tense: 'They (*Somebody*) *stole* the car while I was away.'

In the second example the verb is *not* in the passive voice. The participle is used as an adjective to describe the "*condition*" that the car is stolen. The verb in English cannot be changed into active voice in the same tense.

Key to the Passive Voice

190 The following is a simplified table showing the use of the different passive constructions.

	CONDITION	ACTION, OCCURRENCE
1. *Present tense*	"är" + partic.	s-passive
2. *Past tense*	"var" + partic.	"blev" + partic. *or* s-passive
3. *Present and past perfect*	"har (hade) varit" + partic.	"har (hade) blivit" + partic. *or* s- passive

S-Forms with Reciprocal Meaning

191 The s-form of some verbs can be used to express a reciprocal action:

Vi har *setts* förut.

We have *seen* (*each other*) before.

Vi *träffas* imorgon klockan tio.

We *will meet* (*each other*) tomorrow at ten o'clock.

Vi *möttes* på gatan igår.

We *met* (*each other*) in the street yesterday.

De *följdes åt* hela vägen.

They went together (literally: *accompanied one another*) the whole way.

The reciprocal action can also be expressed by the active form of the verb + "varandra". Cp. § 148.

Deponent Verbs

2 Some verbs always end in -s. They have *passive form* but are *active* in meaning. These are called deponent verbs:

Jag *hoppas*, att han kommer.	I *hope* that he will come.
Han *lyckades* inte få några biljetter.	He did not *succeed* in getting any tickets.
Minns du, när de reste?	Do you *remember* when they left?

Other deponent verbs are: "synas, tyckas" ('seem') "låtsas" ('pretend') "trivas" ('feel at home').

Remarks on the Use of the Auxiliary Verbs

3 att ha

The auxiliary "ha" is often omitted in dependent clauses in the present and past perfect tenses. This is mostly in the written language, e.g.:

Det är en utveckling *som ägt* rum under de sista åren.	It is a development *which has taken* place during the last few years.
Erik märkte snart, att *han kommit* på fel tåg.	Erik soon noticed that *he had got* on the wrong train.

4 att vara, att bli

As a rule, "vara" is equivalent to English 'be'. However, also the verb "bli" ('become, be') can sometimes be used to translate English 'be'. "Bli" is used as the equivalent of English 'be' primarily in the following cases:

1. to form passive voice (cp. §§ 186, 188–190).

Han har *blivit vald* till president.	He has *been elected* President.

2. in expressions of emotion, e.g.:

De *blev glada* (ledsna, lyckliga, förtjusta, etc.).	They *were* (became) *happy* (sorry, happy, delighted, etc.).

3. The present tense of "bli" is often used as a translation of 'will be':

Det blir sent, innan vi kommer dit.	*It will be late* before we get there.
De sa på väderleksrapporten, att *det blir fint* i morgon.	They said on the weather forecast that *it will be fine* tomorrow.

195 ska(ll), skulle

1. "Ska(ll), skulle" are equivalent to English 'shall, will, should, would' used to express future and conditional tense:

Vi *ska träffa* dem imorgon.	We *shall meet* them tomorrow.
De *ska visa* oss staden.	They *will show* us the town.
Jag *skulle hjälpa* dig, om jag kunde.	I *should help* you, if I could.
Skulle det passa dig att äta middag med mig på fredag?	*Would it suit* you to have dinner with me on Friday?

Note 1. Swedish often uses present tense to express the future:

Vi *träffar* dem imorgon.	We *shall meet* them tomorrow.
Jag hoppas ni *får* en skön semester.	I hope you *will have* a pleasant vacation.

Note 2. To express pure future tense Swedish often uses "kommer att" + infinitive instead of "ska":

Vi *kommer att träffa* dem imorgon.	We *shall meet* them tomorrow.
Tror du, att det *kommer att regna* imorgon?	Do you think that it *will rain* tomorrow?

2. "Ska(ll), skulle" are also equivalent to English 'be going to' expressing future tense:

Jag *ska köpa* en ny klänning idag.	I *am going to buy* a new dress today.
Herr Svensson *ska öppna* en ny affär imorgon.	Mr. Svensson *is going to open up* a new shop tomorrow.

3. "Ska(ll), skulle" also correspond to English 'be to' expressing an action which *is to* take place in the future:

Statsministern *ska öppna* kongressen.	The Prime Minister *is to open* the congress.

4. "Ska(ll), skulle" are used as the equivalents of English 'shall, should' to express what a person 'shall, should (ought to)' do:

Du *skall icke stjäla.*	Thou *shalt not steal.*
Ni *skulle inte ha gjort* det.	You *should not have done* it.

196 kan, kunde

"Kan, kunde" have an infinite form "kunna" which corresponds to English 'be able to':

Jag hoppas, att jag *ska kunna* hjälpa dig.	I hope that I *shall be able* to help you.

Note. "Kunna" is also used as a principal verb meaning 'to know' in the sense of 'to have learned, to master' (e.g. a language):

Han *kan* svenska.	He *knows* Swedish.
Kan du din läxa idag?	Do you *know* your lesson today?

197 måste

Note that the same form "måste" is used for English present tense 'must', past tense 'had to' and future 'shall (will) have to':

Jag *måste arbeta* hela dagen idag.	I *must work* all day today.
Jag *måste arbeta* hela dagen igår.	I *had to work* all day yesterday.
Jag *måste arbeta* hela dagen imorgon.	I *shall have to work* all day tomorrow.

198 vill, ville

Swedish "vill" is *seldom* translated by English 'will'. "Vill, ville" are the equivalents of English 'want to, wanted to'. Note, however, that "vill, ville" like the rest of the auxiliary verbs are followed by an infinitive without "att":

De *vill resa* utomlands.	They *want to go* abroad.
Hon *ville se* en annan film.	She *wanted to see* another film.
Jag *skulle vilja ha* en kopp kaffe.	I *should like to have* a cup of coffee.

199 bör, borde

Both present tense "bör" and past tense "borde" correspond to English 'ought to'. Note that "bör, borde" are followed by an infinitive without "att".

Ni *bör resa* till Visby.	You *ought to go* to Visby.
Han *borde ha gjort* det för länge sedan.	He *ought to have done* it long ago.

200 att få

A. "Få" can be *a principal verb* meaning 'get (have), receive':

Kan jag *få* en kopp kaffe?	Can I *get* (have) a cup of coffee?
Jag *fick* brev från henne igår.	I *got* a letter from her yesterday.

B. As *an auxiliary verb* "få" can have several meanings.

1. "Få" corresponds to the English 'may, be allowed to':

Ni *får komma* in nu.	You *may come* in now.
Jag sa, att han *fick göra* det, om han ville.	I said that he *might do* it if he liked.

Vi *får inte röka* här inne.	We *are not allowed to smoke* in here.
De *fick inte tala* med honom.	They *were not allowed to talk* to him.

Note 1. "Får inte" in the present tense and "fick inte" in the past tense are the translations of 'must not':

Vi *får inte röka* här inne.	We *must not smoke* in here.
Han sa, att vi *inte fick röka* här inne.	He said that we *must not smoke* in here.

Note 2. For the different translations of the English 'may' see § 307.

2. "Få" is sometimes used in the sense of "måste" = 'must, have to':

Jag tror, att jag *får gå* till tandläkaren.	I think that I *must go* to the dentist.
Vi *fick vänta* en timme på tåget.	We *had to wait* an hour for the train.

3. "Få höra", "få se", "få veta" have become set verb expressions. "Få höra" and "få veta" are usually translated by 'hear, learn, find out'. "Få se" is usually translated by 'see, discover'.

Jag *fick höra* igår, att hon har gift sig.	I *heard* yesterday that she has got married.
Hon *fick veta* i morse, att de skulle komma.	She *heard* (*learnt*) this morning that they were coming.
Han blev mycket förvånad, när han *fick se* mig.	He was very surprised when he *saw* (*discovered*) me.

C. "Få" is used to render 'make' in the construction 'make somebody do something'. Note that the following infinitive is preceded by "att".

Du *får mig att undra*.	You *make me wonder*.
Vi *fick honom att ge upp* försöket.	We *made him give up* the attempt.

201 att låta

1. "Att låta" corresponds to English 'to let':

Låt oss inte *tala* om det längre.   *Let* us not *talk* about it any longer.

2. "Låta" also corresponds to English 'have, make' in the sense of 'have, make somebody do something', 'have something done':

Jag *lät en målare göra i ordning* köket.   I *had a decorator fix* the kitchen.

De *låter oss arbeta* dag och natt.   They *make us work* day and night.

Du måste *låta klippa håret.*   You must *have your hair cut.*

Vi *lät bygga en simbassäng* förra året.   We *had a swimming-pool built* last year.

202 lär

The auxiliary verb "lär" ('is said to') exists only in the present tense:

Den här filmen *lär vara* mycket bra.   This film *is said to be* very good.

Han *lär ha* mycket pengar.   He *is said to have* much money.

In the past tense 'was said to' is rendered by the Swedish s-passive (§ 185) or by an active construction:

Filmen *sades vara* mycket bra.
Man *sade, att* filmen var mycket bra.   } The film *was said to be* very good.

203 torde

"Torde" expresses a modest request, supposition or likelihood. It corresponds to English 'is probably, will', e.g.:

Detta *torde vara* ett rent undantagsfall.   This *is very probably* an entirely exceptional case.

Det *torde ha varit* omkring klockan fyra.   It *would have been* about four o'clock.

The Infinitive

The Use of "att" before the Infinitive

4 The infinitive in Swedish is sometimes preceded by "att", sometimes not:

Jag lovar *att göra* det.	I promise *to do* it.
Jag tänker *göra* det.	I intend *to do* it.

5 After some verbs, "att" *must* be used, e.g.:

De *kommer att få* en trevlig semester.	They *will get* a nice holiday.
Hon *tycker om att gå* på teatern.	She *likes to go* to the theatre.

6 The infinitive is *not* preceded by "att" *after the modal auxiliary verbs.* These verbs are: *"böra, få, kunna, låta, måste, skola, vilja"*.

Ni *bör köpa* biljetter i förväg.	You *ought to buy* tickets in advance.
Ni *får komma* in nu.	You *may come* in now.
Du *kan tala* svenska.	You *can speak* Swedish.
Hon *måste stanna* hemma.	She *must stay* at home.
Jag *ska fråga* honom.	I *shall ask* him.
Vi *vill gå* på bio.	We *want to go* to the cinema.

7 Also after the following verbs the infinitive, as a rule, is not preceded by "att": *behöva* 'need', *bruka* 'be in the habit of', *hinna* 'have the time to', *orka* 'have the strength to, manage', *synas* 'seem', *tyckas* 'seem', *tänka* 'intend', *våga* 'dare', *ämna* 'intend', *önska* 'wish'. To these verbs can be added a few in the passive voice: *anses* 'be considered to', *påstås* 'be claimed to', *rapporteras* 'be reported to, *sägas* 'be said to'.

Jag *brukar se* honom varje dag.	I *usually see* him every day.
Orkar du *bära* väskan själv?	Do you *manage to carry* the suitcase yourself?
Jag *tänker fråga* henne.	I *intend to* ask her.
Han *anses vara* expert på konst.	He *is considered to be* an expert on art.

208 An infinitive not preceded by "att" *is often used* also after the following verbs:

besluta *decide*	lyckas *succeed*
börja *begin*	låtsas *pretend*
försöka *try*	sluta *finish, stop*
hoppas *hope*	verka *seem*
lova *promise*	vägra *refuse*

Herr Lundberg *beslöt* [*att*] *köpa* en revolver.	Mr. Lundberg *decided to buy* a revolver.
Det *började* [*att*] *regna.*	It *began to rain.*
Du kan *försöka* [*att*] *läsa* en svensk bok.	You can *try to read* a Swedish book.
Det har *slutat* [*att*] *regna* nu.	It has *stopped raining* now.

"För att" Expressing Intention

209 When the English 'to' before an infinitive is equivalent to 'in order to' expressing an intention, it is translated into Swedish by *"för att"*.

Jag sätter på radion *för att* lyssna på nyheterna.	I turn on the radio *to* (*in order to*) listen to the news.
Fru Andersson måste springa *för att hinna med* bussen.	Mrs. Andersson had to run *to* (*in order to*) *catch* the bus.
Hon kom *för att träffa* min far.	She came *to* (*in order to*) *see* my father.

English Infinitive Corresponding to a Full Clause in Swedish

210 In some cases an English infinitive corresponds to a full dependent clause in Swedish, e.g. when the infinitive in English is preceded by an interrogative word:

Jag vet inte, *vad jag ska göra.*	I don't know *what to do.*
Kan ni säga mig, *vart jag ska gå.*	Can you tell me *where to go.*

De hade fått veta, *vem de skulle fråga efter.*	They had been told *whom to ask for.*
Jag är inte säker på, *hur jag ska sköta den här saken.*	I am not sure of *how to handle this matter.*

Translation of English '-ing-forms'

211 For the study of their Swedish equivalents it is important to be able to distinguish between the present participle and the gerund in English, which are identical in form. The difference between them is one of function.

The present participle functions as a verb and as an adjective, the gerund as a noun:

He *came running* to meet me. ⎫
Is there *running* water here? ⎬ (*present participle*)
⎭
Running is good exercise. (*gerund*)

212 There is no **gerund** in Swedish. The English gerund usually corresponds to a Swedish infinitive.

The gerund as the subject of a clause:

Att springa är nyttig motion.	*Running* is good exercise.
Att lära sig ett språk tar lång tid.	*Learning* a language takes a long time.

The gerund as the object in a clause:

Kan du inte *sluta att prata?*	Can't you *stop talking?*
Jag kan inte *låta bli att reta henne.*	I cannot *help teasing her.*

The gerund as the object of a preposition:

Är du *intresserad av att läsa?*	Are you *interested in reading?*
Han ringde *i stället för att skriva.*	He rang *instead of writing.*
Jag lär mig mycket *genom att lyssna.*	I learn a lot *by listening.*

Note. The infinitive can be preceded by a preposition in Swedish.

213 When the gerund is preceded by a possessive word it must be translated into Swedish by a full clause:

Har ni något emot, *att jag röker?*   Do you mind *my smoking?*

Han ville absolut, *att de skulle*   He insisted on *their being punctual.*
komma i tid.

214 As a rule **the present participle** cannot be used as a verb in Swedish. (For the translation of continuous tense see § 221.)

Verbs like 'go, sit, stand, lie' + the present participle usually correspond to two coordinated verbs in Swedish, e.g.:

Han *reser bort och jagar* varje höst.   He *goes away hunting* every autumn.

Jag *satt och läste* en bok.   I *sat reading* a book.

Hon *har gått ut och handlat.*   She *has gone out shopping.*

215 However, after the verb "komma" Swedish uses the present participle:

Han *kom springande* för att möta   He *came running* to meet me.
mig.

216 Abbreviated sentences containing a present participle must be translated into Swedish by full clauses:

Jag träffade två utländska studenter, *som liftade till Kiruna.*   I met two foreign students *hitchhiking to Kiruna.*

Eftersom han är medlem av regeringen, är han väl underrättad.   *Being a member* of the government, he is well informed.

Medan vi bodde där, tittade vi på en del gamla minnesmärken.   *While staying there* we had a look at some old monuments.

217 Note the following construction with 'after':

Efter att ha gått hela vägen, var de mycket trötta.   *After walking* the whole way they were very tired.

'After' + *present participle* in English corresponds to "*efter att ha*" + *supine* in Swedish.

The Use of the Tenses

Present Tense

18 Swedish often uses the present tense in referring to the future.

Hon reser dit i morgon.	*She will go* there tomorrow.
När *kommer hon?*	When *will she come?*
Jag följer dig hem.	*I shall accompany* you home.

Note 1. Swedish uses the present tense in the following cases:

Jag *är född* i juli.	I *was born* in July.
Det *är bäst*, att du gör det genast.	You *had better* do it at once.

Note 2. Present tense of "bli" ('become') is often used to translate 'will be'. For examples see § 194.3.

Past Tense

19 Swedish often uses past tense where English has present. This is especially common in sentences expressing feeling or opinion, e.g.:

Det var synd, att du måste gå.	*It is a pity* that you must go.
Det var tråkigt, att du inte kan komma.	*I am sorry* that you cannot come.
Det var roligt att se dig.	*I am glad* to see you.
Det var dyrt!	*That is expensive!*
Hur var namnet?	*What is your name*, please?

Present Perfect

220 Swedish often uses the present perfect tense where English has past tense. This is found particularly in sentences where there is no definite time indicated and the action belongs completely to the past, and also in sentences containing "någonsin" ('ever') and "aldrig" ('never'), e.g.:

Var *har du lärt dig* att spela bridge?	Where *did you learn* to play bridge?
Vem *har berättat* det för dig?	Who *told* you?
Din fästman *har ringt.*	Your fiancé *telephoned.*
but	
Din fästman *ringde för en timme sedan.*	Your fiancé *telephoned an hour ago.*
Har du någonsin hört någonting så dumt?	*Did you ever hear* such a silly thing?
Jag har aldrig sett något liknande.	*I never saw* anything like it.

Continuous Tense

221 There is no continuous tense in Swedish. The present continuous tense is translated into Swedish by the simple present tense, the past continuous tense by the simple past tense, etc. Thus 'I am writing' and 'I write' are translated in the same way.

Vad *gör du?*	What *are you doing?*
Jag skriver brev.	*I am writing* a letter.
Han arbetade på sin uppsats, när jag kom dit.	*He was working* on his paper when I got there.
Vi har lyssnat på radio hela kvällen.	*We have been listening* to the radio all night.

Note. There is a periphrastic construction which can sometimes be used to render the English continuous tense: "att hålla på och göra något" ('to keep on doing something'), e.g.:

Jag håller på och skriver brev.	*I am writing* a letter.
Han höll på och arbetade på sin uppsats, när jag kom dit.	*He was working* on his paper when I got there.

Reflexive Verbs

222 A verb is called reflexive when the subject and the object are the same person, e.g.:

jag *roar* **mig**	I *amuse myself*
du *roar* **dig**	you *amuse yourself*
han *roar* **sig**	he *amuses himself*
hon *roar* **sig**	she *amuses herself*
den *roar* **sig**	it *amuses itself*
det *roar* **sig**	it *amuses itself*
vi *roar* **oss**	we *amuse ourselves*
ni *roar* **er**	you *amuse yourselves*
de *roar* **sig**	they *amuse themselves*

Note. There are a number of verbs which are reflexive in Swedish but not in English. These are for instance:

beklaga **sig** *complain*, bry **sig** om *care about*, buga **sig** *bow*, föreställa **sig** *imagine*, förlova **sig** *get engaged*, förvåna **sig** *wonder*, gifta **sig** *marry*, känna **sig** *feel*, lägga **sig** *lie down, go to bed*, lära **sig** *learn*, närma **sig** *approach*, raka **sig**, *shave*, röra **sig** *move*, skynda **sig** *hurry*, sätta **sig** *sit down*, ta av **sig** *take off*, ta på **sig** *take on*, tänka **sig** *imagine*, visa **sig** *appear*, vända **sig** *turn*, öva **sig** *practise*.

Compound Verbs

23 A verb to which has been attached a prefix, a noun, an adjective, an adverb or a preposition is called a *compound verb*. Some compound verbs are *inseparable*. This is true of verbs with the prefixes *an-, be-, er-, för-, här-, miss-, sam-, um-, und-, van-, å-*, for instance "betala" ('pay'), "förklara" ('explain'), "samarbeta" ('cooperate').
Other compound verbs are *separable*, e.g. "känna igen" ('recognize'), "kasta bort" ('throw away').

24 Many compound verbs have one separable and one inseparable form with no difference in meaning. The spoken language prefers the separable form. Such verbs are for instance "känna igen, igenkänna", ('recognize'), "lägga ned, nedlägga" ('put down, lay down').

Jag *kände* inte *igen* henne genast.	I did not recognize her at once.
Man *igenkände* henne genast.	People recognized her at once.
Hon *lade ned* två böcker i väskan.	She put down two books in the suitcase.
Presidenten *nedlade* en krans på den berömde författarens grav.	The President laid down a wreath on the tomb of the famous author.

225   Some compound verbs have one separable and one inseparable form which are different in meaning. The inseparable form is generally used in a figurative sense.

Jag har *brutit av* en tand.	I have broken a tooth.
Man har *avbrutit* förhandlingarna.	They have broken off the negotiations.
Jag *gick förbi* honom på gatan.	I walked past him in the street.
Man *förbigick* vissa detaljer med tystnad.	They passed over certain details in silence.

226   Place of the Separable Part of a Compound Verb

The two parts of a separable compound verb sometimes stay together ("Han *kände igen* mig"). Sometimes they are split ("Han *kände inte igen* mig"). At other times the separable part of the verb is added on before the verb ("Ett *igenkännande* leende", literally 'a recognizing smile').

A. In the present and past participle forms the separable part of a compound verb must be added on before the verb.

Hon log ett *igenkännande* leende.	She smiled a smile of recognition.
Det är *bortkastade* pengar.	It is wasted money.
Filmen var mycket *omtyckt*.	The film was very popular.

B. Present and Past Tenses

1. *In independent clauses with normal word order* (Cp. §§ 283–288) the verb and the separable part are split by *aldrig* 'never', *inte*, *icke*, *ej* 'not', and the other adverbs mentioned in § 290.

Han *kände inte igen* mig.	He did not recognize me.
Jag *kastar sällan bort* pengar.	I seldom throw away money.

2. *In independent clauses with inverted word order* the verb and the separable part are split by the subject of the clause.

Kände han igen dig?	Did he recognize you?
Tycker du om kaffe?	Do you like coffee?
Nu *kastar jag bort* de här gamla skorna.	Now I am throwing away these old shoes.

"Aldrig, inte", etc. are placed after the subject in these clauses.

Kände han inte igen dig?	Didn't he recognize you?
Tycker du inte om kaffe?	Don't you like coffee?
Det *talar jag aldrig om* för dig.	I shall never tell you that.

3. *In dependent clauses* "aldrig, inte", etc. must be placed before the verb (Cp. § 290). Thus in these clauses the verb and the separable part stay together.

Jag undrar varför han *inte kände igen* mig.	I wonder why he did not recognize me.
Du vet att jag *sällan kastar bort* pengar.	You know that I seldom throw away money.

C. Compound Tenses

In compound tenses "aldrig, inte", etc, are placed before or after the auxiliary verb and the compound verb is not split.

Han *hade inte känt igen* mig.	He had not recognized me.
Ska du kasta bort skorna?	Are you throwing away the shoes?
Du sade att du *inte skulle kasta bort* skorna.	You said that you would not throw away the shoes.

D. "Bra", "mycket", "illa"

The adverbs *"bra, mycket, illa"* are *always* placed between the verb and the separable part.

De *tycker mycket om* kaffe.	They like coffe very much.
De *tycker illa om* te.	They dislike tea.
Jag vet att de *tycker mycket om* kaffe.	I know that they like coffee very much.
Jag *har alltid tyckt bra om* henne.	I have always liked her very much.

ADVERBS

Adverbs Derived from Adjectives

227 Many adverbs have the same form as the neuter form of the adjective. (For the formation of the neuter form of the adjective see §§ 41, 42.)

Huset är *dåligt* byggt.	The house is *badly* built.
Du kom hem *sent* igår.	You came home *late* yesterday.
Sov *gott!*	Sleep *well!*

228 A few adjectives ending in *-lig* can also form adverbs in other ways:

1. The ending *-en* is added to the *non-neuter* form of the adjective:

antagligen *probably*	troligen *probably*
egentligen *actually*	tydligen *evidently*
möjligen *possibly*	verkligen *really*
slutligen *finally*	

2. The ending *-vis* is added to the *neuter* form of the adjective:

lyckligtvis *fortunately*	naturligtvis *naturally, of course*
möjligtvis *possibly*	troligtvis *probably*
	vanligtvis *usually*

Adverbs Not Derived from Adjectives

In the following groups are mentioned some of the most common adverbs not derived from adjectives.

229 **Simple Adverbs**

1. denoting *time*.

aldrig *never*	då och då *now and then*
alltid *always*	förr *before*
då *then*	genast *at once*

122

ibland *sometimes*	ofta *often*
igen *again*	redan *already*
länge *a long time*	sedan *then, afterwards*
nu *now*	snart *soon*
nyss *just now*	strax *soon, immediately*
någonsin *ever*	sällan *seldom*
när *when*	ännu *still, yet*

2. denoting *place*.

Most of these adverbs have *two* forms. One form is used with verbs of *motion* (indicating direction) and the other form with verbs indicating *rest*.

Adverbs Indicating Rest at a Place	**Adverbs Indicating Motion to a Place**
Var är han?	*Vart* ska han åka?
Where is he?	*Where is he going?*
Bussen stannar **där**.	Går bussen **dit**?
The bus stops there.	*Does the bus go there?*
Har ni varit **här** förr?	Kan du komma **hit**?
Have you been here before?	*Can you come here?*
Jag var **hemma** hela dagen.	Jag gick **hem** klockan fem.
I was at home all day.	*I went home at five o'clock.*

Other adverbs of this kind are:

Indicating Rest at a Place	**Indicating Motion to a Place**
borta *away*	bort *away*
framme *here in front, up here*	fram *forward, up*
inne *in, inside, indoors*	in *in*
nere *down*	ner *down*
uppe *up*	upp *up*
ute *out, outside*	ut *out*

230 Compound Adverbs

A. Adverbs can be formed by a simple adverb + a preposition. Such adverbs are for instance the following,

1. ending in *-ifrån* denoting *motion from a place:*

   därifrån *from there*
   härifrån *from here*
   varifrån *from where*

   De gick *hemifrån* klockan åtta.   They went *from home* at eight o'clock.

2. Ending in *-åt* (after the cardinal points in *-ut*) denoting *motion towards a place:*

bakåt *backwards*	norrut *to the north*
framåt *forwards*	söderut *to the south*
inåt *inwards*	västerut *to the west*
utåt *outwards*	österut *to the east*

   Var god fortsätt *framåt* i vagnen.   Please move *forward* in the carriage.

B. Adverbs can be formed by various endings, e.g.:

-ledes, -lunda, -vis	denoting *manner*
-stans	denoting *place*

Such adverbs are for instance:

således *thus*	naturligtvis *of course*
sålunda *thus*	ingenstans *nowhere*
annorlunda *otherwise*	någonstans *somewhere*
ingalunda *by no means*	(colloquial form: "nånstans")
någorlunda *fairly*	

Note. The expression "Var ... nånstans?" is used in the spoken language as an alternative to the simple "Var?" (*Where?*). It is never necessary to add "nånstans".

Var är min tandborste *nånstans?* *Var* är min tandborste?	*Where* is my tooth-brush?
Vet du, *var* hon är *nånstans?* Vet du, *var* hon är?	Do you know *where* she is?

Cp. the similar expressions in § 122.

1 Participles Used as Adverbs

The present participle is sometimes used as an adverb.
The neuter form of the past participle can also be used as an adverb.

Fröken Lind är *strålande* vacker.	Miss Lind is *radiantly* pretty.
Han lovade *bestämt* att komma.	He *definitely* promised to come.

Comparison of Adverbs

2 Adverbs derived from adjectives have the same comparative and superlative forms as the adjective, e.g.:

kallt *coldly*	kall**are** *more coldly*	kall**ast** *most coldly*
billigt *cheaply*	billig**are** *more cheaply*	billig**ast** *most cheaply*
enkelt *simply*	enkl**are** *more simply*	enkl**ast** *most simply*
högt *highly*	hög**re** *more highly*	hög**st** *most highly*

Note that the 't' of the adverb is dropped before the comparative and superlative endings.

3 A few other adverbs can also be compared:

bra, väl *well*	bättre	bäst
fort *quickly*	fortare	fortast
gärna *gladly*	hellre	helst
illa *badly*	värre	värst
mycket *very*	mer(a)	mest
nära *near*	närmare	närmast
ofta *often*	oftare	oftast

Translation into Swedish of some English Adverbs

234 then

The English 'then' can be translated by "då" or "sedan".

1. 'Then' is translated by "då" when it is equivalent to 'at that time', 'in that case'.

Jag har inte sett henne sedan förra året. Då var hon blond. Får vi fribiljetter? Då kommer jag gärna.	I have not seen her since last year. Then (At that time) she was blond. Do we get free tickets? — Then (In that case) I'll come with pleasure.

2. 'Then' is translated by "sedan" when it is equivalent to 'after that', 'subsequently'.

Först kände jag inte igen honom, men sedan såg jag, att det var min gamla lärare.	At first I did not recognize him, but then (after that) I saw that he was my old teacher.

235 too

1. 'Too' modifying an adjective or an adverb and expressing 'a too high degree of something' is translated by "för (alltför)".

Du är för ung.	You are too young.

2. When it is equivalent to 'also', 'as well', 'too' is translated by "också" or "med".

Detta gäller dig också (med).	This concerns you, too.

236 where

The English 'where' can be an interrogative or a relative adverb.

1. As an interrogative adverb 'where' introduces a direct or indirect question. It is translated by "var" or "vart".

a) *"Var"* is used together with a verb indicating 'rest'.

Var är min penna?	*Where is* my pencil?
Kan ni säga mig, *var* hon *bor?*	Can you tell me *where* she *lives?*

b) *"Vart"* is used together with a verb indicating 'motion'.

Vart gick han?	*Where* did he *go?*
Kan ni säga mig, *vart* den här bussen *går?*	Can you tell me *where* this bus *goes?*

2. As a relative adverb 'where' introduces a relative clause, joining this to a noun in the independent clause. It is translated into Swedish by *"där"* or *"dit"*.

a) *"Där"* is used together with a verb which does *not* indicate motion to the place that 'where' refers back to.

Jag vet en *restaurang, där* man kan både äta och dansa.	I know *a restaurant where* one can both eat and dance.

b) *"Dit"* is used together with a verb which indicates motion to the place that 'where' refers back to.

Jag vet *en restaurang, dit* vi kan gå.	I know *a restaurant where* we can go.

7 yes

The English *'yes'* is translated by *"ja"* or *"jo"*.

1. *"Ja"* is used in answer to a *positive* question.

Har ni varit här förut? — *Ja.*	Have you been here before? — *Yes.*

2. *"Jo"* is used in answer to a *negative* question.

Har ni *inte* varit här förut? — *Jo.*	*Haven't* you been here before? — *Yes.*

CONJUNCTIONS

Coordinating Conjunctions

238 The most common coordinating conjunctions are:

eller *or* så *so*

för *for* ty *for*

men *but* utan *but*

och *and*

239 The coordinating conjunctions introduce *independent* clauses. The subject of an independent clause can be preceded by one of these conjunctions without inversion of word order. See further § 286 under WORD ORDER.

Remarks on the Coordinating Conjunctions

240 *"För"* is the equivalent of 'for' in the spoken language. *"Ty"* is used in the written language.

241 For the translation of the English 'but' see § 297.

242 *"Så"* used as a coordinating conjunction is common in the spoken language.

Jag har inga pengar, *så jag kan inte gå.* I have no money *so I cannot go.*

Subordinating Conjunctions

243 The most important subordinating conjunctions are:

att *that* eftersom *as, since (because)*

då *when* fast(än) *although*

då *as, since (because)* för att *in order that*

därför att *because* förrän *before, until*

innan *before*　　　　　　　sedan *after*
medan *while*　　　　　　　så att *so that*
när *when*　　　　　　　　tills *until*
om *if*　　　　　　　　　　trots att *in spite (of the fact that)*

4 The subordinating conjunctions introduce *dependent* clauses with normal word order. See further § 285 under WORD ORDER.

Remarks on the Subordinating Conjunctions

5 att

1. Like 'that' in English, "att" may sometimes be omitted.

Jag tror, (att) det är en bra　　I think (that) it is a good film.
film.

2. "Att" may be preceded by a preposition. For examples see § 254.

3. Note the use of "att" in conjunctional expressions, e.g. "därför att, för att, trots att".

Varför kom du inte? — *Där-*　Why didn't you come? — *Because*
för att jag var sjuk.　　　　I was ill.

Han gjorde det *trots att vi*　He did it *in spite of our warning*
varnade honom.　　　　　him.

In the last example, the Swedish conjunctional expression introducing a full dependent clause renders the English prepositional phrase 'in spite of' + a gerund (cp. § 213).

4. Note that 'that' in English may also be a demonstrative or a relative pronoun. For the different translations of 'that' see § 302.

46 då — när

1. "Då" and "när" are interchangeable as temporal conjunctions = 'when'.

Då (När) det regnar, stannar　*When* it rains we stay at home.
vi hemma.

2. "Då" can also be a causal conjunction meaning 'as, since, because'. It is then interchangeable with "eftersom".

Då (Eftersom) det regnade,   *As* it was raining, we stayed at
stannade vi hemma.   home.

Translation into Swedish of Some English Subordinating Conjunctions

247 **after:** see § 295.

248 **as**

1. 'as' = 'since' = "*eftersom (då)*".

Eftersom han inte kommer, måste   *As he does not come* something must
någonting ha hänt.   have happened.

2. 'as' = 'while' = "*bäst som, medan, (som)*".

Bäst som jag stod där, kom en flicka   *As I stood there*, a girl came run-
springande.   ning.

3. In other cases = "*som*".

Som barn var han mycket blyg.   *As a child* he was very shy.
Det låter *som om* det regnar.   It sounds *as if* it is raining.

249 **as — as**

1. Comparison in an affirmative clause: "*lika — som*".

Han är *lika gammal som jag*.   He is *as old as I* (am).

2. In other cases: "*så — som*".

Han är inte *så gammal som* han ser   He is not *as (so) old as* he looks.
ut.

Note the idiom "*så snart (som)*" ('as soon as').

Jag ska komma *så snart (som)* jag är   I am coming *as soon as* I am ready.
färdig.

250 **before:** see § 296.

51 **that:** see § 302.

52 **until**

'Until' is rendered both by *"förrän"* and *"tills"*.

1. After an affirmative clause "tills" is always used.

De väntade, *tills* vi kom.   They waited *until* we came.

2. After a negative clause 'until' is rendered by "förrän" when it can be replaced by 'before'.

De ville inte gå, *förrän* vi kom.   They did not want to go *until* (*before*) we came.

PREPOSITIONS

Remarks on the Use of Prepositions in Swedish

253 In Swedish, as opposed to English, an infinitive can be preceded by a preposition.

Herr Lundberg är mycket intresserad *av att läsa.*	Mr. Lundberg is very interested *in reading.*
Han gick in i rummet *utan att knacka.*	He entered the room *without knocking.*

254 In Swedish a dependent clause beginning with "att" ('that') can be preceded by a preposition. In translation into English the preposition is usually dropped; if the preposition is retained, some expression like 'the fact that' is usually inserted after it.

Jag är *övertygad om att* han kan göra det.	I am *convinced that* he can do it.
Jag är *säker på att* vi får vackert väder.	I am *sure that* we shall have fine weather.
De *klagar över att* Sverige har vänstertrafik.	They *complain about the fact that* Sweden has left-hand traffic.

255 In many cases when a preposition is used in Swedish English does not use one:

1. before a complement of the predicate. The most common preposition used in Swedish is "till".

Vi *döpte* pojken *till* Karl.	We *christened* the boy Charles.
Han *utnämndes till* utrikesminister.	He *was appointed* Foreign Secretary.
Hon *valdes till* medlem av första kammaren.	She *was elected* a member of the First Chamber.

2. in expressions like the following where the preposition precedes 'parts of the body'.

Han skakade *på* huvudet.	He shook his head.
Hon ryckte *på* axlarna.	She shrugged her shoulders.
Tvätta dig *om* händerna!	Wash your hands!
Tvätta dig *i* ansiktet!	Wash your face!
Han var våt *om* fötterna.	His feet were wet.

56 In many cases when a preposition is used in English Swedish does not use one. Note particularly the following cases:

1. There are no equivalents of the prepositions '*at*' before hours, '*in*' before years, and '*on*' before dates.

Möt mig *klockan fem*.	Meet me *at five o'clock*.
Han är född *1935*.	He was born *in 1935*.
Han är född *den 17 mars 1935*.	He was born *on March 17, 1935*.

2. There is no equivalent of the English '*to*' after the following verbs:

Båten *tillhör* oss.	The boat *belongs to* us.
Har detta aldrig *hänt* dig?	Has this never *happened to* you?
Det *tycks* mig, som om jag hade sett honom förut.	It *seems to* me that I have seen him before.

3. In certain cases there is no equivalent of the English '*of*'. See further § 280.

Kan jag få *en kopp kaffe*.	May I have *a cup of coffee*.

The Use of Some Common Prepositions

257 av

1. For "av" as a translation of '*of*' following a noun see § 278.

2. "Av" is used as a translation of the English '*of*' to express the material of which something is made.

Den här statyn är *gjord av brons*. (This statue is *made of bronze*.)

3. "Av" corresponds to 'by' to express the agent.

Landet *besökes av* många turister. (The country *is visited by* many tourists.) Hästen *blev skrämd av* en bil. (The horse *was frightened by* a car.)

4. "Av" corresponds to 'from' after verbs like the following.

Hon *dog av* hjärtslag. (She *died from* stroke.) Jag ska *få* boken *av* min far. (I shall *get* the book *from* my father.) Jag *har köpt* pennan *av* min bror. (I *have bought* the pencil *from* my brother.) Jag kan *låna* en rock *av* honom. (I can *borrow* a coat *from* him.)

5. "Av" corresponds to 'with' to express the 'cause' in phrases like the following.

Hon var *vit av köld*. (She was *white with cold*.) Han var *röd av ilska*. (He was *red with anger*.)

6. Note also the expression:

Han är *intresserad av* att läsa. (He is *interested in* reading.)

258 efter

1. As a rule "efter" is used to translate 'after'.

Vi dricker alltid kaffe *efter lunch*. (We always have coffee *after lunch*.)

2. "Efter" is used to translate 'for' in expressions like the following.
Vem ska jag *fråga efter*? (Whom shall I *ask for*?)
Du måste *leta efter* dina skor. (You must *look for* your shoes.) Jag *längtar efter* något gott att äta. (I *long for* something good to eat.) Vi måste *ringa efter* doktorn. (We must *call for* the doctor.) Vi måste *skicka efter* doktorn. (We must *send for* the doctor.)

259 framför

1. As a rule "framför" is used to translate 'in front of'.

Vi parkerade bilen *framför huset*. (We parked the car *in front of the house*.)

2. Note the use of "framför" after the verb "föredra".
Jag *föredrar* öl *framför* vin. (I *prefer* beer *to* wine.)

3. "Framför" is used to translate 'above' in the following expression:
Framför allt måste ni läsa mer svenska. (*Above all* you must read more Swedish.)

⁵0 från

1. As a rule "från" is used to translate 'from'. When the preposition is stressed it often has the form "ifrån".

Vi fick *ett vykort från Visby*. (We got *a postcard from Visby*.) Hon *gick ifrån mig*. (She *left me*.)

Note 1. 'From' is sometimes rendered by "av". For examples see above under "av", 4.

Note 2. In the following case 'from' has no equivalent in Swedish:

Hon är *olik dem*. (She is *different from* them.)

61 för

1. "För" sometimes corresponds to 'for'.

Han är lång *för sin ålder*. (He is tall *for his age*.)

Note. In §§ 258 and 273 are given instances of "efter" and "åt" as translations of 'for'. See also the discussion of the translation of 'for' as a preposition of time in § 275.

2. "För" after adjectives.

Är du *rädd för* råttor? (Are you *afraid of* rats?) Det är *typiskt för* honom. (That's *typical of* him.) Det är *nytt för* mig. (That's *new to* me.)

3. "För" after verbs.

Jag måste *gömma* den *för* henne. (I must *hide* it *from* her.) Han *intresserar sig för* det mesta. (He *takes an interest in* most things.) Man *anklagar* honom *för* stöld. (He is *accused of* stealing.) Man *misstänker* honom *för* brottet. (He is *suspected of* the crime.) Vi måste *varna* honom *för* detta. (We must *warn* him *of* [*against*] this.) Du måste *berätta för* mig om hennes man. (You must *tell me* about her husband.) Hon *förklarade* det *för* mig. (She *explained* it *to* me.) Han blev *presenterad för* fröken Lind. (He was *introduced to* Miss Lind.)

²62 för — sedan

"För – sedan" is used to translate 'ago'. "För" is placed before the object of the preposition and "sedan" after the object.

Vi kom till Sverige *för två månader sedan*. (We came to Sweden *two months ago*.)

263 genom

1. As a rule "genom" is used to translate 'through'. When the preposition is stressed it often has the form "igenom".

   Han körde *genom staden*. (He drove *through the town*.) Han ögnade *igenom* tidningen. (He *glanced through* the paper.)

2. "Genom" also corresponds to 'by' in the sense of 'because of, thanks to, by means of'.

   Han stoppade tåget *genom att dra* i nödbromsen. (He stopped the train *by pulling* the emergency brake.)

264 hos

There is no separate preposition in English which corresponds directly to "hos".

1. As a preposition of place "hos" is often translated by 'with', 'at ...'s (house)'.

   Jag bodde *hos min moster* förra året. (I stayed *with my aunt* last year.) Vi var *hos Nordkvists* igår kväll. (We were *at the Nordkvists'* last night.) Jag var *hos doktorn* (*tandläkaren*) i morse. (I was *at the doctor's* (*the dentist's*) this morning.)

2. "Hos" is also used in a more abstract sense in expressions like the following in which English has 'in, about, with'.

   Det finns ingen fruktan *hos honom*. (There is no fear *in him*.) Detta står att läsa *hos Homeros*. (This can be read *in Homer*.) Felet ligger *hos mig*. (The fault is *with me*.)

265 i

A. *"I" as a Preposition of Place*

1. As a rule "i" is used to translate 'in' as a preposition of place.

   Hon är född *i Sverige*. (She was born *in Sweden*.) Bor du *i Stockholm?* (Do you live *in Stockholm?*) Det finns två stolar *i rummet*. (There are two chairs *in the room*.)

   See also § 299 about the translation of 'in' as an adverb.

2. "I" is also used to translate 'into' as a preposition of place.

▌ Han föll *i vattnet*. (He fell *into the water*.) Jag kan inte få *i mitt huvud*, att det var han. (I can't get it *into my head* that it was him.)

3. Sometimes "i" is used to translate 'at', e.g. before names of towns and villages.

Han föddes *i Norwich*. (He was born *at Norwich*.)
Note also the following expressions in which 'at' is rendered by "i":
Hon är *i kyrkan* [*i skolan*]. (She is *at church* [*at school*].)

4. Note also the following similar expressions in which "i" renders 'to':

Hon *går i kyrkan* varje söndag. (She *goes to church* every Sunday.)
Jag *går i skolan* varje dag. (I *go to school* every day.)

5. "I" is sometimes used to translate 'on' as a preposition of place.

Sitt inte *i gräset*. (Don't sit *on the grass*.) Jag hörde honom tala *i* [på] *radio* häromdagen. (I heard him speak *on the radio* the other day.) Jag såg ett bra program *i* [på] *TV* igår. (I saw a good programme *on TV* yesterday.) Han talar *i telefonen* just nu. (He is speaking *on the telephone* just now.)

Note also the instances given of "i" as a translation of 'of' in § 279.

B. *"I" as a Preposition of Time*
Note that "i" is *not* used to translate 'in' as a preposition of time. For the translation of 'in' as a preposition of time, see § 276.

1. "I" is used in expressions of time to answer the question 'how long'; it thus corresponds to the English 'for'. See also § 275.

Jag har studerat svenska *i tre månader*. (I have studied Swedish *for three months*.)

2. "I" corresponds to the English 'to' in expressions of time like the following.

Klockan är *fem* [*minuter*] *i sex*. (It is *five* [*minutes*] *to six*.)

3. "I" is used to translate 'at' in the following expressions.

Den första snön kom *i början* [*i slutet*] *på december*. (The first snow came *at the beginning* [*the end*] *of December*.) Hjälpen kom *i sista ögonblicket*. (The help came *at the last moment*.)

4. "I" is used in the following common expressions of time. In several of them there is no corresponding preposition in English.

I förrgår, igår, idag, imorgon, i övermorgon (the day before yesterday, yesterday, today, tomorrow, the day after tomorrow).

I natt, i morse, i eftermiddag, i kväll, i natt (last night, this morning, this afternoon, this evening [tonight], tonight).

5. "I" is used without any equivalent in English in the following expressions:

a) to express past time (It is then followed by a noun in an old possessive form.):

for the seasons and festivals: *i vintras, i våras, i somras, i höstas (last winter, last spring, last summer, last autumn)*; *i julas, i påskas (last Christmas, last Easter)*

for the days of the week: *i måndags, i tisdags*, etc. *(last Monday, last Tuesday, etc.)*

b) to express present or future time:

for the seasons and festivals: *i vinter, i vår, i sommar, i höst (this winter, this spring, this summer, this autumn)*; *i jul, i påsk (this Christmas, this Easter)*

c) in the expressions:

en gång i sekunden [i minuten, i timmen, i veckan, i månaden] (once a second [a minute, an hour, a week, a month]).

Note, however, *"en gång **om** året" (once a year)*, *"en gång **om** dagen (once a day).*

C. *"I" after Certain Adjectives*

Hon är *duktig i* svenska. (She is *good at* Swedish.) Jag är *förtjust i* choklad. (I am *fond of* chocolate.) Han *blev kär i* henne vid första ögonkastet. (He *fell in love with* her at first sight.)

266   med

1. As a rule "med" is used to translate 'with'.

Ät inte *med fingrarna.* (Don't eat *with your fingers.*) Borta *med vinden.* (Gone *with the Wind.*)

2. "Med" is used to translate 'by' to express the means of transportation.

Ska du fara *med båt* eller *med tåg*? (Are you going *by boat* or *by train*?) De fick ett brev *med posten*. (They got a letter *by mail*.)

3. "Med" after certain adjectives (or participles).

Han är *förlovad med* henne. (He is *engaged to* her.) Han är *gift med* hennes syster. (He is *married to* her sister.) Han är *släkt med* kungen. (He is *related to* the King.)

4. "Med" after certain verbs.

Vad kan han *mena med* det? (What can he *mean by* that?) Hon ska *förlova sig med* honom imorgon. (She is going to *get engaged to* him tomorrow.) Han *gifte sig med* sin kusin. (He *married* his cousin.) Kan jag få *tala med* herr Persson? (May I *speak to* Mr. Persson?)

67 mot

1. "Mot" is used to translate both 'against' and 'towards'. It sometimes has the form "emot".

Regnet piskade *mot fönstren*. (The rain was beating *against the winows*. De kom springande *mot mig*. (They came running *towards me*.) De gick *i riktning mot* staden. (They walked *in the direction of* [*towards*] the town.) Detta är [*e*]*mot mina principer*. (This is *against my principles*.) *Har ni något emot att* jag röker? (*Do you mind* [lit.: have you anything against] my smoking?) Jag blev trött *mot slutet av* föredraget. (I got tired *towards the end of* the lecture.)

2. After certain adjectives expressing 'conduct' "mot" corresponds to the English 'to'.

Han är mycket *artig mot* sin fru. (He is very *polite to* his wife.) Han är mycket *snäll mot* henne. (He is very *kind to* her.) Han är alltid *vänlig mot* sin rika moster. (He is always *kind to* his rich aunt.)

3. "Mot" after certain verbs.

Vi måste *byta* vår våning *mot* en större. (We must *exchange* our flat *for* a bigger one.) Hon *log mot* honom. (She *smiled at* him.) Hur kan man *skydda sig mot* kylan? (How can one *protect oneself from* the cold?)

268 om

1. As a rule, "om" can be used to translate 'about'.

Han har skrivit *en bok om Sverige*. (He has written *a book about* [on] *Sweden*.) Jag har inte sett filmen, men jag har *läst om den*. (I have not seen the film, but I have *read about it*.)
However, when 'about' is used as an adverb with hours or figures to express 'around, approximately' it is translated by "omkring".
Han kom *omkring klockan åtta*. (He came *about eight o'clock*.) Boken kostar *omkring femton kronor*. (The book costs *about fifteen crowns*.)

2. Adjectives or adverbs + "om".

Ska vi ställa bordet *till höger* eller *till vänster om* soffan? (Shall we put the table *to the right* or *to the left of* the sofa?) Hon var *medveten om* sitt misstag. (She was *conscious of* her mistake.)
Without equivalent in English:
Hon var *kall* [*varm*] *om* händerna. (Her hands were cold [warm].) Är du *torr* [*våt*] *om* fötterna? (Are your feet dry [wet]?)

3. Verbs + "om".

Hon *bad mig om* litet vatten. (She *asked me for* some water.) Gissa vad jag *drömde om* i natt. (Guess what I *dreamt of* last night.) Han *påminner* mig *om* någon. (He *reminds* me *of* someone.) Hon var *övertygad om* hans oskuld. (She was *convinced of* his innocence.) Boken *handlar om* svensk litteratur. (The book *deals with* [*is about*] Swedish literature.)

4. "Om" as a preposition of time

a) Corresponding to English 'in'. (See also § 276.1.)

Jag ska resa hem *om två dagar*. (I am going home *in two days*.) Han kommer *om en timme*. (He is coming *in an hour*.)

b) Used interchangeably with "på" before the seasons, days and parts of the day. English in this case has 'in'. "Om" is not so common as "på" in these expressions; it is used more in formal and poetic language.

Det är vackert *om våren* [*om sommaren, om hösten, om vintern*]. (It is pretty *in the spring* [*in the summer, in the autumn, in the winter*].)
Det är varmt *om dagarna* och kallt *om kvällarna*. (It is warm *in the daytime* and cold *in the evenings*.)

c) Without any equivalent in English in the following expressions.

Han ringer *en gång om dagen*. (He calls *once a day*.) Vi reser dit *en gång om året*. (We go there *once a year*.)

For the expressions 'once a week, once a month' see under "*i*".

259 på

A. "*På*" *as a Preposition of Place*

1. As a rule "på" is used to translate 'on' as a preposition of place.

   Jag har mattor *på golvet*. (I have carpets *on the floor*.) Ställ vasen *på bordet*. (Put the vase *on the table*.)

2. In some expressions "på" corresponds to 'in'.

   Vi möttes *på gatan*. (We met *in the street*.) Såg du någon *på gården?* (Did you see anybody *in the court[yard]*?) Det finns inte ett moln *på himlen*. (There is not a cloud *in the sky*.) Vi har varit *på landet*. (We have been *in the country*.) Jag har aldrig varit *på den här platsen [på det här stället]*. (I have never been *in this place*.)

3. "På" corresponds to 'at' in expressions like the following.

   Vi var *på bio* igår. (We were *at the pictures* [went to the movies] yesterday.) Vilket *hotell* bor han *på?* (What *hotel* is he staying *at?*) Jag ska fråga *på kontoret*. (I shall ask *at the office*.) Jag såg en bra pjäs *på teatern* igår. (I saw a good play *at the theatre* yesterday.) Han mötte mig *på stationen*. (He met me *at the station*.)

4. "På" is used to translate 'to' in expressions like the following.

   Vi *gick på bio* igår kväll. (We *went to the pictures* [movies] last night.) Vi ska gå *på konsert [på Operan, på teatern]* i kväll. (We are *going to a concert [to the Opera, to the theatre]* tonight.)

B. "*På*" *as a Preposition of Time*

Note that the English 'on' before dates has no equivalent in Swedish. See § 256.1.

1. "På" renders 'on' before the weekdays.

   På söndag [morgon] ska jag resa till Göteborg. (*On Sunday [morning]* I am going to Gothenburg.) Jag kommer tillbaka *på tisdag*. (I shall be back *on Tuesday*.)

2. "På" is used to translate 'in' before the seasons and parts of the day. Cp. § 268.4.b.

På vintern [*på våren, på sommaren, på hösten*]. (*In* [*the*] *winter, in* [*the*] *spring, in* [*the*] *summer, in* [*the*] *autumn.*) *På morgonen, på eftermiddagen, på kvällen.* (*In the morning, in the afternoon, in the evening.*)

Other expressions in which "på" renders the English 'in':

På nittonhundratalet. (*In the 20th century.*) *På artonhundranittiotalet.* (*In the eighteen-nineties.*)

For further instances of "på" rendering 'in' see § 276.2.

3. For instances of "på" rendering 'for' as a preposition of time see § 275.2.

C. "På" after Certain Adjectives

Han är *blind på* ena ögat. (He is *blind of* one eye.) Staden är *rik på* minnesmärken. (The town is *rich in* monuments.) Han är *säker på* segern. (He is *sure of* his victory.) Jag är *trött på* hans historier. (I am *tired of* his stories.) Varför är hon *arg* [*ond*] *på* dig? (Why is she *angry with* you?)

D. "På" after Certain Verbs

Får jag *bjuda* dig *på* något? (May I *offer* you something?) Vi *hoppas på* bättre väder. (We are *hoping for* better weather.) Jag *hör på* nyheterna varje morgon. (I *listen to* the news every morning.) Du kan *lita på* mig. (You can *trust* me.) Herr Karlsson *ropar på* servitrisen. (Mr Karlsson *calls* [*for*] the waitress.) *Se på* honom. (*Look at* him.) Jag *tror på* spöken. (I *believe in* ghosts.) *Tänk på* all tid du förlorar. (*Think of* all the time you lose.) *Vänta på* mig. (*Wait for* me.)

Note also the instances of "på" rendering the English 'of' given in § 279.

270 till

A. "Till" as a Preposition of Place

1. As a rule "till" is used to translate the English 'to'.

De ska resa *till Lappland.* (They are going *to Lapland.*) Hur långt är det *från Stockholm till Malmö?* (How far is it *from Stockholm to Malmö?*)

2. Note the use of "till" after the verbs "anlända, komma fram" ('arrive at' or 'in').

Hur dags *kommer vi fram* [*anländer vi*] *till Stockholm?* [*till Södertälje*]? (What time do we *arrive in Stockholm* [*at Södertälje*]?)

3. "Till" corresponds to 'for' in the following expressions.

Är det här *tåget till Karlstad?* (Is this *the train for* Karlstad?) *Båten till Göteborg* går om en timme. (*The boat for Gothenburg* leaves in an hour.)

B. *"Till" as a Preposition of Time*

1. As a rule "till" corresponds to the English 'to', sometimes to 'till' as a preposition of time.

De var här *från* den första *till* den femte december. (They were here *from* the first *to* the fifth of December.) Låt oss vänta *till i morgon.* (Let us wait *till tomorrow.*)

2. "Till" renders 'for' in expressions like the following:

Läxan till idag var lång. (*The lesson for today* was long.) Finns det några biljetter *till i kväll?* (Are there any tickets *for tonight?*) Ska ni resa bort *till jul?* (Are you going away *for Christmas?*) Kom inte för sent *till middan* idag. (Don't be late *for dinner* today.)

3. The following expressions with "till" are used interchangeably with "i höst, i vinter, i vår, i sommar" to express future time.

Vi ska flytta in i det nya huset *till hösten* [*till vintern, till våren, till sommaren*]. (We shall move into the new house *this autumn* [*this winter, this spring, this summer*].)

4. Note the use of "till" in the expression "till sist" ('at last, finally').

Det var svårt att övertyga honom, men vi lyckades *till sist.* (It was difficult to convince him, but *finally* we succeeded.)

C. *"Till" after Certain Verbs*

Vad *används* den här maskinen *till?* (What is this machine *used for?*) Vi *gratulerade* henne *till* segern. (We *congratulated* her *on* her victory.) Kan du *översätta* det här *till* svenska? (Can you *translate* this *into* Swedish?) Note the use of "till" before a complement of the predicate discussed in § 255.1.

D. *Other Expressions with "till"*

Stenen restes *till minne av* skolans grundare. (The stone was raised *in memory of* the founder of the school.) Jag känner henne *till namnet.* (I know her *by name.*) Vi köpte varorna *till ett pris av* en krona stycket. (We bought the goods *at the price of* one crown a piece.)

In a number of set expressions with "till" the preposition is followed by a noun in the possessive case, e.g.:

Sitta *till bords* (sit *at table*), gå *till fots* (walk), gå *till sjöss* (go *to sea*), gå [*ligga*] *till sängs* (go *to* [*be in*] *bed*).

Note also the instances of "till" rendering 'of' given in § 279.

271 under

A. *"Under" as a Preposition of Place*

"Under" corresponds to 'under' and 'below' as a preposition of place and in a figurative sense.

Väskan ligger *under sängen*. (The suit-case is *under the bed*.) Temperaturen här är sällan *under noll*. (The temperature here is seldom *below zero*.) Det är *under hans värdighet*. (It is *below his dignity*.)

B. *"Under" as a Preposition of Time*

1. As a rule "under" corresponds to 'during'.

   Ingen är hemma *under dagen*. (Nobody is at home *during the day*.) Detta hände *under kriget*. (This happened *during the war*.)

2. Sometimes "under" corresponds to 'for' or 'in [the course of]'.

   Under två veckor var de helt isolerade. (*For two weeks* they were completely isolated.) Stora förändringar ägde rum *under hans regering*. (Great changes took place *in his reign*.) Två nya förslag lades fram *under förhandlingarna*. (Two new proposals were put forward *in the course of the negotiations*.)

3. Note the expression *"under tiden"* ('*meanwhile, in the meantime*').

272 vid

A. *"Vid" as a Preposition of Place.*

1. Often "vid" corresponds to 'at' in English as a preposition of place. Han mötte mig *vid stationen*. (He met me *at the station*.) Karin studerar *vid universitetet*. (Karin is studying *at the university*.)

2. Sometimes "vid" corresponds to 'by' in the sense of 'at the side of'. Kom och sitt *vid brasan*. (Come and sit *by the fire*.) Vi hade en underbar dag *vid havet*. (We had a wonderful day *by the sea*.)

3. "Vid" also corresponds to 'on' in the sense of 'at the side of'.
Huset ligger *vid vägen*. (The house stands *on the road*.) Newcastle ligger
vid floden Tyne. (Newcastle stands *on the river Tyne*.) Göteborg ligger
vid havet. (Gothenburg is situated *on the sea* [*on the coast*].)

B. *"Vid" as a Preposition of Time*

1. Note that 'at' before hours in English has no equivalent in Swedish.
See § 256.1.

2. However, "vid" corresponds to 'at' in the following expressions:
Han kom hem *vid midnatt*. (He came home *at midnight*.) Kan du komma
vid 8-tiden? (Can you come *around* [*at about*] *eight o'clock?*) Var var ni
vid denna tidpunkt? (Where were you *at this time?*) Han blev kung *vid
arton års ålder*. (He became King *at the age of eighteen*.)

3. "Vid" sometimes corresponds to 'on' in the sense of 'immediately after'.
Vid framkomsten till staden fann de, att invånarna övergivit den. (*On
their arrival* at the town they found that the inhabitants had deserted it.)
"Vid" also corresponds to 'on' in the following expression:
Jag var inte närvarande *vid detta tillfälle*. (I was not present *on this
occasion*.)

C. *"Vid" after Certain Adjectives*
Jag är [o]van *vid* den här maskinen. (I am [un]used *to* this machine.)

D. *"Vid" after Certain Verbs*
"Vid" is used corresponding to 'to' after verbs like "tie to, fasten to'.

Stolarna på båten var *fästade vid* golvet. (The chairs on the boat were
fastened to the floor.)

73 åt

A. *"Åt" as a Preposition of Place.*

Han gick *åt* det där hållet. (He went *in that direction*.) Rummet ligger *åt*
norr. (The room *faces the north*.)

B. *"Åt" Expressing the Dative.*

In this case "åt" is, as a rule, interchangeable with "till' as a translation
of 'to'.

Ge den *åt* [*till*] *honom*. (Give it *to him*.)

"Åt" is also used to translate 'for'

Kan du köpa boken *åt mig?* (Can you buy the book *for me?*) Jag ska göra det *åt dig*. (I shall do it *for you*.)

C. *Other Examples of the Use of "åt"*.

Hon var *glad åt* [*över*] presenten. (She was *pleased with* [*happy about*] the gift.) *Skratta* inte *åt mig*. (Don't *laugh at* me.) Han *ägnar sig åt* studier. (He *devotes himself to* studies.)

274 över

1. "Över" corresponds to 'over, above, across'.

   Han är *över åttio år* gammal. (He is *over eighty years* old.) Det är tre grader *över noll*. (It is three degrees *above zero*.) Hunden sprang *över gatan*. (The dog ran *across the street*.)

2. "Över" is used to translate 'past' in the following expressions of time.

   Klockan är *fem* [minuter] *över sex*. (It is *five* [minutes] *past six*.) Klockan är *över åtta*. (It is *past eight o'clock*.)

3. "Över" is used after the following adjectives.

   Är du *förvånad över* resultatet? (Are you *surprised at* the result?) Jag är *glad över* det. (I am *glad* [*happy*] *about* it.) Jag är *stolt över dig*. (I am *proud of* you.)

   Note also the instances of "över" rendering 'of' given in § 279.

Translation into Swedish of 'for' and 'in' as Prepositions of Time

275 *'For' as a Preposition of Time*

1. In a positive clause 'for' is usually translated by "i" or "under". Like 'for' "i" and "under" can often be omitted.

   Jag har varit här *i två dagar*. (I have been here *for two days*.) Jag ska stanna [*i, under*] *två månader*. (I shall stay [*for*] *two months*.)

2. In a negative clause 'for' is usually translated by "på".

   Jag har inte varit där *på två år*. (I have not been there *for two years*.) Jag har inte sett henne *på länge*. (I have not seen her *for a long time*.)

76 *'In'* as a Preposition of Time.

1. 'In' is translated by "om" to answer the question 'when ...?' in a clause expressing future action.

Jag ska resa hem *om två veckor.* (I am going home *in two weeks.*) Han kommer *om en timme.* (He is coming *in an hour.*)

2. 'In' corresponds to "på" in expressions like the following to answer the question 'How long does it take [to do it]'?

Du kan läsa boken *på en dag.* (You can read the book *in a day.*) Han kan göra det *på några timmar.* (He can do it *in a couple of hours.*)

Translation of a Prepositional Phrase with 'of' Following a Noun

77 *'Of'* Rendered by Swedish Possessive in *'s'*.

The English possessive construction with 'of' is usually rendered by the Swedish s-possessive. (Cp. §§ 35–37.)

Blommans färg	The colour *of the flower*
Lampans storlek	The size *of the lamp*
Bokens innehåll	The contents *of the book*

Often the Swedish possessive in -s can be exchanged for a prepositional phrase; 'of' is then usually translated by a preposition other than "av". See further below § 279.

78 *'Of'* Translated by "av".

1. To express a picture, an image, etc. of somebody or something.

Det här är *ett porträtt av Karl XII.* (This is *a portrait of Charles XII.*) I parken står *en staty av skolans grundare.* (In the park there is *a statue of the founder of the school.*)

In the definite form these expressions are often interchangeable with a possessive in -s.

Har du läst *'Dorian Grays porträtt'?* (Have you read *'the Portrait of Dorian Gray'?*)

2. In the expressions 'king of, queen of' etc.

Vad heter *kungen av Norge?* (What is the name of *the King of Norway?*)

3. After words denoting 'parts of' something.

Han fick *hälften* [*en tredjedel*] *av* pengarna. (He got *half* [*a third*] *of* the money.) *I denna del av staden* har jag aldrig varit förut. (In *this part of the town* I have never been before.)

4. To express an objective relation. (The word following 'of' is the object of the word preceding it.)

Befrielsen av staden kom på våren 1944. (*The liberation of the town* came in the spring of 1944.) På partiets program står *avskaffandet av dödsstraffet*. (On the party's programme is *the abolition of death penalty*.)

These expressions with "av" can as a rule be replaced by a possessive in -s. "*Befrielsen av staden*" = "*stadens befrielse*", "*avskaffandet av dödsstraffet*" = "*dödsstraffets avskaffande*".

279   '*Of*' *Translated by Prepositions Other Than* "*av*".

In other cases than those given above in § 278, 'of' usually corresponds to prepositions other than "av". Below are given some common instances.

'of' = "för"

Han var *föremål för* allas beundran. (He was *the object of* everybody's admiration.) Han har en underbar *känsla för* humor. (He has a wonderful *sense of* humour.) Han är *representant för* ett amerikanskt bolag. (He is *the representative of* an American company.)

'of' = "på"

Kommer du ihåg *färgen på* huset? (Do you remember *the colour of* the house?) Han kan *namnen på* alla franska städer. (He knows *the names of* all French towns.) Detta var *slutet på* historien. (This was *the end of* the story.) Har du givit upp *tanken på* din bok? (Have you given up *the thought of* your book?)

'of' = "i"

Han är *borgmästare i* Nacka. (He is *Mayor of* Nacka.) Hon är *professor i engelska*. (She is *professor of English*.) Jag måste bättra på mina *kunskaper i italienska*. (I must brush up my *knowledge of Italian*.)

'of' = "till"

Det här är *dörren till* badrummet. (This is *the door of* the bathroom.) Han är *son till* rektorn. (He is *the son of* the Headmaster.) Det här är

en vän till mig. (This is *a friend of mine.*) Vad var *orsaken till* branden?
(What was *the cause of* the fire?)

'of' = "vid"

När stod *slaget vid* Waterloo? (When was *the Battle of* Waterloo?)

'of' = "över"

Vi köpte *en karta över* Holland. (We bought *a map of* Holland.) Har du
en lista över [*på*] namnen? (Have you *a list of* the names?)

80 *'Of' without Equivalent in Swedish.*

'Of' has no equivalent in Swedish:

1. after words denoting quantity.

   En kopp kaffe (*a cup of* coffee), *en bit* bröd (*a piece of* bread), *ett glas*
   vatten (*a glass of* water), *en ask* choklad (*a box of* chocolates), *ett kilo*
   socker (*a kilo of* sugar), *ett par* handskar (*a pair of* gloves), *en flaska* vin
   (*a bottle of* wine).

   Note the expressions: *Vi var fyra* [*stycken*]. (*There were four of us.*)
   Jag vill ha *tre* [*stycken*]. (I want *three of them.*)

2. after geographical appellations:

   Kungariket Danmark (*The Kingdom of* Denmark.) *Staden* Stockholm
   (*The city of* Stockholm.) *Ön* Malta (*The Island of* Malta.)

3. after the names of seasons and festivals and certain words, e.g. 'month',
   'title'.

   Sommaren 1955. (*The summer of* 1955.) *Påsken* 1958. (*The Easter of* 1958.)
   Månaden maj [or, more often "maj månad"] (*The month of* May.) Han
   fick *titeln* hertig av Halland. (He got *the title of* Duke of Halland.)

4. in expressions of date.

   [*Den*] *första* maj (*The first of* May) [*Den*] *sista* april (*The last of* April)

5. in the expressions 'kind of', 'manner of', 'sort of'. The corresponding
   Swedish words are in the possessive case:

   Ett nytt *slags* material. (A new *kind of* material.) *Alla sorters* människor.
   (*All sorts of* people.)

6. after the word "hela" and the names of the cardinal points.

   Jag ska vara borta *hela april*. (I shall be away *the whole of April.*) Vi bor
   i *södra Stockholm*. (We live in *the south of Stockholm.*)

281 Translation of 'to'

A. 'To' as a Preposition.

1. 'To' is usually translated by "till". For examples see those given under "till" in § 270.

2. In expressions of time like the following 'to' corresponds to "i". *Klockan är fem [minuter] i sex.* (It is *five [minutes] to six.*)

B. 'To' as a Particle Marking the Infinitive.

1. In infinitive phrases it corresponds to "att". *Att fela* är mänskligt. (*To err* is human.)

2. After verbs it usually corresponds to "att". "Att" can often be omitted (cp. §§ 207, 208).

Jag *lovar [att] göra* det. (I *promise to do* it.) Han *vägrade [att] tala.* (He *refused to speak.*)

3. After some verbs 'to' has no equivalent (cp. §§ 206, 207).

Vad *tänker du göra?* (What do you *intend to do?*) Vi *borde gå* dit. (We *ought to go* there.) De *tycks vara* nöjda. (They *seem to be* pleased.) Jag *vill gå* hem. (I *want to go* home.)

C. 'To' Used as a Shortened Form of 'in order to' (Expressing Intention). (cp. § 209.)

In this case 'to' corresponds to "för att" in Swedish.

Han *gick för att öppna* dörren. (He *went to open* the door.) Jag satte på radion *för att höra* nyheterna. (I turned on the radio *to hear* the news.)

282 Index for the Translation of Some English Prepositions

Below are given the main ways of translating some common English prepositions. The numbers refer to the pages where examples of these translations are given.

below: under 144;

by: av 134, genom 136, med 139, vid 144;

during: under 144;

for: efter 134, för 135, i 137, 146, på 146, till 143, under 144, åt 146;

from: av 134, från 135;

in: av 134; hos 136; i 136, om 140, 147, på 141, 142, 147, till 142, 144;

into: i 137, till 143;

of: av 133, 147, för 135, 148, i 148,

om 140, på 142, 148, till 148, vid 149, över 146, 149;

on: i 137, på 141, vid 145;

over: över 146;

past: över 146;

through: genom 136;

to: i 137, med 139, mot 139, på 141, till 142, 143, vid 145, åt 145, 146;

towards: mot 139;

under: under 144;

with: av 134, hos 136, med 138, 139.

WORD ORDER

The Place of the Subject

Introduction

283 The question of normal word order or inverted word order in Swedish offers difficulties to English-speaking students.

By *normal word order* is meant that the subject is placed before the verb. English as a rule has normal word order in statements, e.g.:

I *was* there yesterday. — Yesterday I *was* there.

By *inverted word order* is meant that the subject is placed after the verb (in compound tenses after the auxiliary verb). It is the usual word order in questions. English sometimes has inverted word order in statements.

Where *is she?* — Here *is my sister.*

284 The question of word order in Swedish is connected with the distinction between independent and dependent clauses.

Word Order in Dependent Clauses

285 Dependent clauses *always* have normal word order.

Dependent clauses can be introduced by:

a) subordinating conjunctions. (See § 243).

b) relative pronouns (§§ 88–94) and relative adverbs (§ 236.2).

c) interrogative pronouns (see §§ 112–123) and interrogative adverbs (§ 236.1) in reported speech.

Jag vet, *att han är* hemma.	I know *that he is* at home.
Jag vet inte, *när han kom* hem.	I don't know *when he came* home.
Jag vet inte, *om han har varit* hemma länge.	I don't know *if he has been* at home for a long time.
Jag känner hans moster, *som bor* i Kiruna.	I know his aunt *who lives* in Kiruna.

Han reste till Kiruna, *där han hälsade på* sin moster.	He went to Kiruna *where he visited* his aunt.
Jag vet inte, *vad han gjorde* igår.	I don't know *what he did* yesterday.
Jag vet inte, *varför han kom* hem så sent igår.	I don't know *why he came* home so late yesterday.

Note. "Om" which introduces a conditional clause can sometimes be omitted. The word order is then inverted. This is sometimes the case in English, too.

Har jag inte kommit kl. 8, ska ni inte vänta på mig.	*If I have not come* by 8 o'clock you should not wait for me.
Vore jag i ditt ställe, skulle jag inte göra det.	*Were I* in your place I should not do it.

Word Order in Independent Clauses

Independent clauses sometimes have normal word order, sometimes inverted word order.

86 *Normal word order* is used in independent clauses when the subject begins the clause (the subject can be an interrogative pronoun).

Note that an independent clause can be introduced by "för, men, och, ty, utan" (coordinating conjunctions).

Herr Lundberg har en gammal bil.	*Mr Lundberg has* an old car.
Vem har min penna?	*Who has* my pencil?
Jan hade en penna *och Anita hade* ett kuvert, *men de hade* inget frimärke.	*Jan had* a pencil *and Anita had* an envelope *but they had* no stamp.

87 *Inverted word order* is used in independent clauses *when a word other than the subject begins the clause* (the subject, however, may be preceded by a coordinating conjunction).

The subject is then preceded by a complement of the verb.

This complement can be:

a) an adverb or adverbial phrase:

Nu **är han** hemma.	*Now* **he is** at home.
Igår kväll **kom han** hem kl. 8.	*Last night* **he came** home at 8 o'clock.

b) the object in the clause:

Det **vet jag** säkert.	*That* **I know** for certain.
Någon ost **har jag** inte köpt.	**I have** not bought *any cheese*.

Note that the object may be a *direct quotation*.

"Har du läst den här boken?" **frågade han.**	*"Have you read this book?"* **he asked.**

288 *Inverted word order* is also used when the independent clause is preceded by a dependent clause:

När vi kom, **var han** inte hemma.	*When we came* **he was** not at home.

The Place of the Adverb

289 *In independent clauses* adverbs must be placed after the verb (in compound tenses after the auxiliary verb) unless they start the sentence. Cp. § 287 a.

Jag *dricker aldrig* kaffe.	I *never drink* coffee.
Jag *har aldrig druckit* kaffe.	I *have never drunk* coffee.
Aldrig trodde jag det var sant.	*Never did I believe* it was true.
Jag *tror nästan* att hon är sjuk.	I *almost believe* that she is ill.
Hon *stängde tyst* dörren.	She *quietly closed* the door.

290 In *dependent clauses* a number of adverbs must be placed before the verb (in compound tenses before the auxiliary verb). Such adverbs are for instance: *aldrig* never, *inte, icke, ej* not (negative adverbs), *alltid* always, *ofta* often, *redan* already, *snart* soon, *sällan* seldom (adverbs expressing indefinite time), *antagligen* probably, *gärna* willingly, *kanske* perhaps, *möjligen* possibly.

Du vet att jag *aldrig dricker* kaffe.	You know that I *never drink* coffee.
Du vet att jag *aldrig har druckit* kaffe.	You know that I *have never drunk* coffee.
Har du hört varför hon *inte* kom?	Have you heard why she *did not come?*
Tror ni att de *redan kan ha gått?*	Do you think that they *may already have gone?*
Han säger att han *gärna skulle* komma.	He says that he *would be glad to come.*

Thus while in English these adverbs stay in the same position in independent and dependent clauses they change their place in Swedish. Note particularly the very common case of *"inte"*.

Independent clause:

Han **är inte** hemma.	He *is not* at home.

Dependent clause:

Jag vet att han **inte är** hemma.	I know that he *is not* at home.

Note. Concerning the place of these adverbs together with a compound verb see § 226.

91 However, other adverbs, for instance those expressing more definite time and those denoting place, are placed after the verb also in dependent clauses.

Han säger att han *kommer imorgon.*	He says that he *will come tomorrow.*
Du vet att vi *måste gå nu.*	You know that we *must go now.*
Har ni sett om han *är här?*	Have you seen if he *is here?*
Vet du om hon *är hemma?*	Do you know if she *is at home?*

292 When one of the adverbs mentioned in § 290 is found in an *independent clause with inverted word order* it is placed after the subject.

Är han **inte** hemma nu?	*Isn't he* at home now?
Har du **inte** *läst* den här boken?	*Haven't you read* this book?
När vi kom, *var han* **inte** hemma.	When we came *he was not* at home.

293 The adverbs "*inte* [*icke, ej*], *aldrig, alltid*" are placed between "att" and the infinitive ('split infinitive'). Other adverbs may be placed either between "att" and the infinitive or after the infinitive.

Han bad mig *att inte göra* det.	He asked me *not to do* it.
Han bad mig *att genast komma.*	He asked me *to come at once.*

or

Han bad mig *att komma genast.*

APPENDIX

Translation into Swedish of Some English W
that Need Special Attention

294 An English word which can appear as different parts of speech is often rendered by more than one word in Swedish. It is very common in English that a word is used both as a noun and as a verb (e.g. 'change, drink, fight, help, promise, rain, use, walk'). As a rule, Swedish has different forms for the noun and the verb ('promise', for instance, as a noun is "löfte" as a verb "lova"). In other cases, a certain English word may be used as an adverb, a conjunction, or a preposition, each part of speech requiring a separate translation. In most cases of this type sufficient information is provided in dictionaries. However, some points which may be difficult to find in dictionaries are discussed below. The rules given do not aim at presenting a comprehensive analysis of the problems. The purpose is that of providing some practical hints for translation.

After

295 The English 'after' may be a conjunction or a preposition. As a conjunction (i.e. when it is possible to replace 'after' by 'when' or 'since') it is translated by "sedan" or "efter det att". As a preposition it is rendered by "efter".

Sedan han hade rakat sig, gick han på bio.   *After he had shaved* he went to the movies.

Efter nyår ska jag sluta röka.   *After New Year's Day* I shall stop smoking.

Before

296 The English 'before' may be an adverb, a conjunction, or a preposition.

1. Adverb. 'Before' may be replaced by 'earlier', 'previously'. Swedish: "förr", "förut", or "tidigare" (these three words are usually interchangeable).

Jag har aldrig varit här *förr* (*förut, tidigare*).   I have never been here *before*.

157

2. Conjunction. 'Before' is rendered by "innan" except when it is preceded by a negative clause in which case "förrän" is the most common translation.

Vi talade med honom, *innan han reste.*	We spoke to him *before he left.*
Det dröjde inte länge *förrän han ringde mig.*	It wasn't long *before he called me.*

3. Preposition.

a) Referring to time. 'Before' may be replaced by 'previous to'. Swedish: "före".

b) Referring to place. 'Before' may be replaced by 'in front of'. Swedish: "framför" (sometimes "inför").

Jag träffade honom strax *före jul.*	I saw him just *before Christmas.*
Vi satt *framför brasan.*	We were sitting *before the fire.*
Plikten *framför allt.*	Duty *before everything* [*above all*].

But

297 The English 'but' may be a coordinating conjunction or a preposition.

1. As a coordinating conjunction 'but' can be translated by "men" or "utan".

a) After an affirmative clause it is always translated by "men".

Våningen är bra, *men* den är liten.	The apartment is good, *but* it is small.

b) After a negative clause 'but' corresponds to "men" when the second statement does not contradict the first. If this second statement contains a verb it is often possible to insert 'in spite of that' after 'but'.

Han är inte född i Sverige, *men* han talar svenska som en infödd.	He was not born in Sweden, *but* [in spite of that] he speaks Swedish like a native.

c) After a negative clause 'but' corresponds to "utan" when the second statement contradicts the first.

De är inte rika *utan* fattiga.	They are not rich *but* [on the contrary] poor.

2. As a preposition 'but' can usually be translated by "utom".

Alla hus utom ett brann ner.   *All the houses but one* bur

Either

298 The English 'either' may be a pronoun, an adverb, or a coordinating conjunction.

1. Pronoun.
   a) 'Either' means 'both'. Swedish: "båda".
   b) 'Either' means 'any', 'anybody', 'anyone'. Swedish: "vem som helst" or "vilken som helst", if the basic meaning of the clause is affirmative; "någon" or "någondera", if the basic meaning is negative (cp. §§ 131, 133, 135).

   I *båda* fallen.   In *either* case.
   Vem som helst av er får ta den.   *Either* of you may take it.
   Jag känner *inte någon[dera]* av dem. I don't know *either* of them.

2. Adverb. Swedish: "heller".

   Min far är på kontoret, och min   My father is at the office and my
   mor är *inte* hemma *heller*.   mother is *not* at home *either*.

3. Coordinating conjunction. The English 'either ... or' is in Swedish "antingen ... eller".

   Han är *antingen* svensk *eller* norr- He is *either* a Swede *or* a Norwe-
   man.   gian.

In

299 The English 'in' may be a preposition or an adverb.

1. Preposition (of place). Swedish: "i" (for the translation of 'in' as a preposition of time see § 276).

   Hur länge har ni varit *i Sverige?*   How long have you been *in Sweden?*

2. Adverb. Swedish: "in" or "inne" (cp.} 229.2.).

Jag måste *lämna in* min uppsats i morgon.	I must *hand in* my paper tomorrow.
Jag *var inte inne*, när han sökte mig.	I *wasn't in* when he came to see me.

One

300 The English 'one' may be a numeral or a pronoun.

1. Numeral. Swedish: "en" (neuter: "ett").

Det finns bara *ett hotell* i staden.	There is only *one hotel* in the town.

2. Pronoun.

a) 'One' means 'you', 'people', 'a person'. Swedish: "man" (possessive: "ens"; object form: "en"; cp. § 138.).

Man kan inte arbeta i den här hettan.	One can't work in this heat.

b) 'One' is used in English as a substitute for a certain noun implied or occurring elsewhere in the context. In Swedish there is usually no equivalent to this 'one'. Sometimes, however, it is rendered by "(en) sådan".

Fru Olsson hade en blå klänning och fröken Asp *en skär*.	Mrs. Olsson wore a blue dress and Miss Asp *a pink one*.
Han är officer, men han ser inte ut som *en sådan*.	He is an officer but he doesn't look like *one*.
Jag tycker inte om den här hatten; jag vill ha *den där* i stället.	I don't like this hat; I want *that one* instead.

c) The English 'the one' is "den" or "det". The English 'the ones' is "de".

Jag vill ha den där boken. — Vilken? — *Den* som jag pekar på.	I want that book. — Which one? — *The one* I am pointing at.

Note 1. 'One another' is "varandra": "Varför hjälper ni inte *varandra*?" ('Why don't you help *one another*?')

Note 2. 'One' used as a contrast to 'the other' or 'another' is "den ena, det ena": "De hade två döttrar; *den ena* var ljus och *den andra* var mörk." ('They had two daughters; *one* was blond and *the other* was dark-haired'.).

Since

1 The English 'since' may be a conjunction, a preposition or an adverb.

1. Conjunction.

   a) 'since' = 'after' = "*sedan*"

Jag har inte sett henne, *sedan* hon kom tillbaka.	I have not seen her *since* she came back.

   b) 'since' = 'as, because' = "*eftersom*"
   Ex.: see *as*, § 248.

2. Preposition: "*sedan*".

Han har inte skrivit *sedan i julas*.	He has not written *since Christmas*.

3. Adverb: 'since' = 'since that time' = "*sedan dess*".

Vad har du gjort *sedan dess?*	What have you been doing *since?*

That

2 The English 'that' may be a demonstrative pronoun, a relative pronoun, or a conjunction.

1. Demonstrative pronoun. Swedish: "den där" (neuter: "det där") or "den" (neuter: "det") (cp. §§ 95, 96, 98).

Jag förstår inte *det där ordet.*	I don't understand *that word.*
Har du inte hört *den historien?*	Haven't you heard *that story?*
Det visste jag inte.	I didn't know *that.*

2. Relative pronoun ('that' may be replaced by 'which' or 'who(m)'). Swedish: "som" (or "vilken"; cp. §§ 88, 89).

Han använder *en bil, som* tillhör någon annan.	He is using *a car that* belongs to somebody else.

3. Conjunction. Swedish: "att".

Hon sade, *att hon var förkyld.*	She said *that she had a cold.*
Jag visste inte, *att hon var sjuk.*	I didn't know *that she was ill.*

Time

303 The English noun 'time' is rendered by two different nouns in Swedish: "tid (-en, -er)" and "gång (-en, -er)". "Gång" should be used whenever 'time' is used in the sense of 'occasion', "tid" in other cases (*e.g.* when 'time' means 'period of time').

Jag ska påminna honom om det *varje gång* jag träffar honom.	I shall remind him of it *every time* I see him.
Hon talade inte till mig *en enda gång* den kvällen.	She didn't speak to me *a single time* that evening.
Vi kan inte stanna här *någon längre tid*.	We cannot stay here for *any great length of time*.
Kom ni *i tid* till middagen?	Did you come *in time* for the dinner?
Tiderna var annorlunda i min ungdom.	*Times* were different in my youth.

Verbs

Ask

304 When the English 'ask' means 'request', 'beg', the Swedish equivalent is "be" (past tense: "bad"; supine: "bett"; a longer infinitive form "bedja" is sometimes used in the written language).

When 'ask' means 'ask a question', 'inquire' it is rendered by "fråga" (1st conj.).

Har du *bett honom göra det?*	Have you *asked him to do it?*
Har du *frågat honom om* han har gjort det?	Have you *asked him if* he has done it?

Get

305 The English 'get' is used in some ten different meanings from the Swedish point of view. The following might be regarded as the three basic cases.

a) 'Get' means 'receive'. Swedish: "få (fick, fått)".

b) 'Get' means 'arrive'. Swedish: "komma (kom, kommit)".

c) 'Get' means 'become', 'grow'. Swedish: "bli (blev, blivit)".

Fick du några presenter på din födelsedag?	*Did you get any presents* on your birthday?
Vi *kom inte dit* i tid.	We *didn't get there* in time.

| Han *blev ond.* | He *got angry.* |
| Han börjar *bli gammal.* | He is *getting old.* |

Know

06 The English 'know' is usually "veta (visste, vetat)" in Swedish but there are two important exceptions: 1) 'Know a person' is "känna (kände, känt) en person"; 2) 'Know' in the sense of 'to have learned, to master' (*e.g.* a language) is "kunna (kunde, kunnat)".

Vet du var han bor?	*Do you know* where he lives?
Känner du fröken Ström?	*Do you know Miss Ström?*
Kan du tyska?	*Do you know German?*
Varför *kunde han inte sin läxa?*	Why *didn't he know his lesson?*

07 **May**

1. 'May' when expressing possibility, uncertainty is translated by "kunna".

| Det *kan* vara sant. | It *may* be true. |
| Han *kan* komma när som helst. | He *may* come any time. |

2. 'May' used in polite questions is translated by "kunna få" or "få lov".

Kan jag få tala med herr S.?	*May I speak to* Mr. S.?
Kan jag få titta på din nya bok?	*May I look* at your new book?
Får jag lov att ringa?	*May I phone?*

3. 'May' expressing permission is translated by "få".

| Ni *får* komma in nu. | You *may* come in now. |
| Jag sa, att han *fick* göra det, om han ville. | I said that he *might* do it if he liked. |

08 **Tell**

1. 'Tell' in the sense of 'relate', 'tell a story' is "berätta" (1st conj.).

2. 'Tell' in the sense of 'inform' is "tala om för" (1st conj.) or "säga (sade, sagt)".

3. 'Tell' in the sense of 'ask', 'request', 'exhort' is "säga åt" or "säga till". In this case 'tell' is often followed by an infinitive ('tell somebody to do something').

Du får inte *berätta sådana historier,* när barnen hör på.	You must not *tell* (*relate*) *such stories* when the children are listening.
Han *talade om för* mig [Han *sade* mig,] att han skulle gifta sig.	He *told* (*informed*) me that he was going to marry.
Jag *sade åt* honom [Jag *sade till* honom] att ringa efter en taxi.	I *told* (*asked, requested*) him to call for a taxi.

Think

309 The English 'think' may be rendered by "tänka" (2nd conj.), "tro" (3rd conj.), or "tycka" (2nd conj.).

1. "*Tänka*" renders 'think': 1) when 'think' means 'ponder', 'contemplate', 'use one's brains', and 2) when 'think' is followed by 'of' ('think of ...' = "tänka på ...").

Jag kan inte *tänka* i det här oväsendet.	I cannot *think* in this noise.
Det *tänkte* jag inte *på.*	I didn't *think of* that.

2. "*Tro*" renders 'think' when 'think' means 'believe'.

Jag *tror* inte att han vinner den här matchen.	I don't *think* (*believe*) he will win this match.
Vi *trodde* att de kunde höra oss.	We *thought* they could hear us.

3. "*Tycka*" renders 'think' when 'think' means 'find' (i.e. when it is used to express a personal opinion or taste). In comparison with "tro", "tycka" contains less of contemplating and more of perception through one's senses.

Min man *tycker* att den här fisken smakar illa.	My husband *thinks* that this fish has a bad taste.
Tycker du inte att det är vackert här?	Don't you *think* it is pretty here?
Jag *tycker* att hans föreläsningar är intressanta.	I *think* his lectures are interesting. (Speaking from experience.)
but	
Jag *tror* att hans föreläsningar är intressanta.	I *think* his lectures are interesting. (I have not attended them but I believe they are interesting.)

INDEX

The numbers refer to pages.

"Swedish Phrasebook" 1972
(Middlesex England) Penguin #3358

Tack så mycket

Tack ska du ha för idag
N!